National 4 & 5

Religious, Moral and Philosophical Studies

Joe Walker
Kate Jenkins

HODDER GIBSON
AN HACHETTE UK COMPANY

Joe Walker would once again like to thank Lorna and David for their support.

Grateful thanks to Joe for inviting me to do this book and showing me the ropes; to Alistair and Amy Jenkins for putting up with my many absences from their weekends; and Annie McSwan for being my rock at school, and teaching me about Buddhism.

And in loving memory of my dear Mum, who always encouraged me to think about the big questions.

The Publishers would like to thank the following for permission to reproduce copyright material:

Photo credits

Section opener image on **p.1** © Marina Karkalicheva – Fotolia.com; **p.7** (left) © British Humanist Association, www.humanism.org.uk, www.richarddawkins.net, (right) © FrankBirds – Fotolia.com; **p.8** © Eric Gevaert – Fotolia.com; **p.10** (top) © Shawn Hempel – Fotolia.com, (bottom) © Online Bible Foundation UK; **p.11** (right) © karam miri – Fotolia.com; **p.13** (top) © DXfoto.com – Fotolia.com, (centre left) © Distinctive Images – Fotolia.com, (centre right) © LOOK Die Bildagentur der Fotografen GmbH / Alamy; **p.17** © Dinodia Photos / Alamy; **p.19** © Ints Vikmanis – Fotolia.com; **p.20** © Adrian Sherratt / Alamy; **p.22** (top) © ArTo – Fotolia.com, (bottom) © Hackenberg-Photo-Cologne / Alamy; **p.23** (left) © Gamma-Keystone via Getty Images, (right) © British Humanist Association, www.humanism.org.uk, www.richarddawkins.net; **p.25** (left) © Paylessimages – Fotolia.com, (right) © PhotoAlto / 27 Objects; **p.26** (top) © Marina Karkalicheva – Fotolia.com, (bottom) © javarman – Fotolia.com; **p.28** © Coprid – Fotolia.com; **p.29** (bottom left) © iko – Fotolia.com, (top right) © Imagestate Media (John Foxx) / Vol 03 Nature & Animals, (centre right) © Studiotouch – Fotolia.com; **p.31** © Photonika – Fotolia.com; **p.32** © Getty Images; **p.33** (left) © reflektastudios – Fotolia.com, (right) © kotafoty – Fotolia.com; Section opener image on p.39 © Design Pics – Thinkstock; **p.40** (left) © Julie Jacobson/AP/Press Association Images, (right) © Design Pics – Thinkstock; **p.42** © Frank Gärtner – Fotolia.com; **p.54** (left) © Michael Matisse/Photodisc/ Getty Images/ Science, Technology & Medicine 2 54, (right) © Laurent Hamels – Fotolia.com; **p.55** © 1989 Roger Ressmeyer/ NASA/CORBIS; **p.56** © moodboard / Alamy; **p.57** (left) © Everett Collection Historical / Alamy, (right) © minemero – Thinkstock; **p.61** © North Wind Picture Archives / Alamy; **p.63** © rabbit75_fot – Fotolia.com; **p.65** © VINCENT MONCORGE/LOOK AT SCIENCES/SCIENCE PHOTO LIBRARY; Section opener image on p.67 © Xavier – Fotolia.com; **p.71** © EMILIO SEGRE VISUAL ARCHIVES/AMERICAN INSTITUTE OF PHYSICS/SCIENCE PHOTO LIBRARY; **p.72** (left) © EMILIO SEGRE VISUAL ARCHIVES/ AMERICAN INSTITUTE OF PHYSICS/SCIENCE PHOTO LIBRARY, (right) © pialhovik – Thinkstock.com; **p.73** (right) © PETER TUFFY, UNIVERSITY OF EDINBURGH/SCIENCE PHOTO LIBRARY; **p.77** (right) © NJ – Fotolia.com; **p.78** © Mary Evans Picture Library; **p.83** (left) © nickolae – Fotolia.com, (right) © DAVID PARKER/SCIENCE PHOTO LIBRARY; **p.85** (left) © Xavier – Fotolia.com, (right) © demarfa – Fotolia.com; **p.86** © Alexandr Mitiuc – Fotolia.com; **p.88** © Marcio Silva – Thinkstock; **p.89** © kohy – Fotolia.com; **p.90** (top) © PASCAL GOETGHELUCK/SCIENCE PHOTO LIBRARY, (left) © SCOTT CAMAZINE/SCIENCE PHOTO LIBRARY, (right) © NATURAL HISTORY MUSEUM, LONDON/SCIENCE PHOTO LIBRARY, (bottom) © PASCAL GOETGHELUCK/SCIENCE PHOTO LIBRARY; **p.91** © Mikhail Markovskiy – Fotolia.com; **p.94** (left) © Creation Museum (CreationMuseum.org), (right) © *Creation* magazine, Creation Ministries International; **p.96** (right) © Radu Razvan – Fotolia.com; Section opener image on p.101 © FrankBirds – Fotolia.com; **p.102** © Tyler Olson – Fotolia.com; **p.105** © NEW YORK PUBLIC LIBRARY/SCIENCE PHOTO LIBRARY; **p.107** (left) © INTERFOTO / Alamy, (right) © National Geographic Image Collection / Alamy; **p.108** © Mike Goldwater / Alamy; **p.109** © SIMON FRASER/ SCIENCE PHOTO LIBRARY; **p.111** © Job (oil on canvas), Bonnat, Leon Joseph Florentin (1833-1922) / Musee Bonnat, Bayonne, France / Giraudon / The Bridgeman Art Library; **p.113** © S McTeir; **p.115** © Leo Lintang – Fotolia.com; **p.116** © AFP/Getty Images; **p.117** © REX/Sipa Press; **p.118** © age fotostock / Alamy; **p.120** © Snakes and Ladders - the path to heaven or hell, mid 18th century, . / © Royal Asiatic Society, London, UK / The Bridgeman Art Library; **p.122** © Photononstop / SuperStock; **p.123** © Patrick – Fotolia.com; **p.124** (top) © eroticshutter – Fotolia.com, (bottom) © Bullit Marquez/AP/Press Association Images; **p.125** © mdfiles – Fotolia.com; **p.126** (left) © REX, (right) © British Humanist Association, www.humanism.org.uk, www.richarddawkins.net.

Every effort has been made to trace all copyright holders, but if any have been inadvertently overlooked the Publishers will be pleased to make the necessary arrangements at the first opportunity.

Orders: please contact Bookpoint Ltd, 130 Park Drive, Abingdon, Oxon OX14 4SE. Telephone: (44) 01235 827720. Fax: (44) 01235 400454. Lines are open 9.00–5.00, Monday to Saturday, with a 24-hour message answering service. Visit our website at www.hoddereducation.co.uk. Hodder Gibson can be contacted direct on: Tel: 0141 848 1609; Fax: 0141 889 6315; email: hoddergibson@hodder.co.uk

© Joe Walker and Kate Jenkins 2014

First published in 2014 by

Hodder Gibson, an imprint of Hodder Education,

An Hachette UK Company

2a Christie Street

Paisley PA1 1NB

Impression number	5 4 3 2 1
Year	2018 2017 2016 2015 2014

Cover photo © Sergey Nivens – Fotolia.com

Illustrations by Barking Dog Art Illustration and Design

Typeset in FS Albert Pro 11.5/14.5 by Integra Software Services Pvt. Ltd.

Printed in Italy

A catalogue record for this title is available from the British Library

ISBN: 978 1444 187 410

Contents

The problem of evil and suffering 101

This textbook is a little different from previous RMPS textbooks. The 'information' about each of the topics is so widely available these days, especially online, that it makes little sense to include pages of information here. What teachers need are stimuli to engage learners and encourage active responses to learning, preparing learners not just to learn and retain stuff (though that's not without value), but to actively engage with material so that they can apply the skills of learning in completely new contexts. Learners need to learn to become their own teachers – with guidance at first, of course.

They need to be empowered to take on their own learning, and be able to cope with the amount of information that is available to them nowadays. It's probably fair to say that they have technology in their pockets that could teach them more than you or we ever could in a lifetime. But they have to be able to handle this information intelligently, separating fact from fiction, opinion from truth, objectivity from propaganda, and so on.

This textbook aims to assist learners in actively engaging with religious and philosophical questions in line with the requirements of the SQA courses at National 4 and 5. The active learning and engagement processes used in this book are, it is to be hoped, automatically differentiated, as well as being stimulating and challenging. They are designed to help learners to understand the course material and so to succeed in the exam, but they're also designed to spark a lifelong interest in the topics under examination, which will grow and develop throughout life.

The materials rely heavily on the skills identified in Bloom's Taxonomy and the authors hope this textbook will stimulate all levels of thinking from the lowest to the highest order thinking identified by Bloom below:

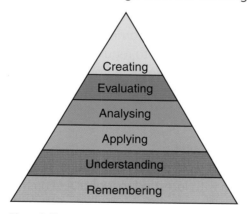

Bloom's Taxonomy

The authors would not presume to instruct teachers how to teach, but we should recognise that both the introduction of *Curriculum for Excellence* and the new National Qualifications in RMPS presuppose new and innovative approaches to learning and teaching that are more active and engaging, while of the highest quality. Joe Walker has become a recent convert to collaborative learning approaches, and after almost 30 years of teaching this is proof that an old dog can learn new tricks! Actively involving learners in their own learning has so many benefits for teachers and learners, it's hard to list them all; and the research is quite unambiguous in the conclusion that active learning far surpasses the passive stuff of years gone by. Your classroom will be noisier, but it will also be more productive.

We would, however, like to propose some suggestions that will maximise the effective use of this textbook.

- Teacher talk in lessons should be carefully analysed so that the balance between learning and teaching is clear and varied.
- Class seating arrangements should be varied and allow for different learning and teaching styles. This could be negotiated with learners, but should be organised so as to maximise creative discussion and activity.
- Lessons should include variety of approach and should include clear shared learning intentions and reviewed success criteria. Learners should be on the 'learning journey' with you, not stumbling in the dark. Teachers and learners should recognise that learning processes might involve making mistakes, but that this can itself be a stepping stone along the route to successful learning.
- Learners should keep a reflective learning log of their activities; this is an elegant and purposeful solution to the 'problem' of homework!
- Technology should be used in class, but not just by the teacher (e.g. death by PowerPoint®). Learners should be encouraged to carry out research and use technology to assist their learning (texting questions to others in class?). They should also use technology to respond to activities.
- All learners should be involved in and engaged with learning, fulfilling roles suited to their talents and abilities, which may vary according to the task.
- Dissemination of learners' learning should be encouraged beyond the classroom, for example, talking with parents, other learners, teachers, members of the community and faith communities are all to be encouraged.
- The language of learning should be shared with learners, not held as a symbol of power by teachers. Bloom's Taxonomy, for example, can be referred to regularly, assisting learners in understanding the learning process which, research confirms, improves learning.
- At the end of each lesson, everyone involved should know what they were trying to achieve and to what extent they achieved it. If it was not achieved, then all should be able to reflect upon why this was so and how this might be put right.
- Learning and teaching should be informed by research. Teachers should be learners themselves and prepared to abandon things that don't work and try out things that are out of their comfort zone. They should match up their own teaching with latest educational research findings so that a learner's experience of school (or a subject) isn't just based on the lottery of the habits and assumptions their teacher has.

We hope this book will be of use to you and your learners.

Joe Walker and Kate Jenkins

The existence
of God

1 Exploring the existence of God 1: biblical views of God

Source 1

'The God of the Old Testament does seem to have a varied personality. He can be angry, jealous, keen to take revenge on people for not doing what he wants them to do; in some ways, his behaviour is quite odd. He creates a beautiful garden for the life he creates, and tells them that everything they want will be provided for them. He gives them freedom, but then he tells them not to eat fruit from one tree. Now, we all know human nature; if you tell someone not to do something, then that's the very thing they probably want to do. So they eat the fruit, God gets annoyed, banishes them from the garden and punishes them for all eternity. It looks like the freedom he gave them wasn't actually freedom at all. Later on, he helps armies to utterly destroy their enemies, and he picks on one man – poor old Job – who's just trying to get on with his life, and puts him through some rotten experiences to test him out or something like that. I don't really get that God.'

Source 2

'Yes, the God of the Old Testament does seem to behave rather strangely at times but we have to remember that the Bible was written by people – and it was written by people who were trying to make a point in different times and different places, so we have to be careful about stringing it all together and trying to build up a picture of God which makes sense. The picture of God is an odd mish-mash of views about gods generally. We can't apply our twenty-first-century rules about what gods should and shouldn't do to the past; that doesn't make sense … and anyway, Jesus showed us later what God was really like.'

Activity 1

1 Read through the creation stories in Genesis 1 and 2. In groups, take each of the following statements and think about what evidence in the stories links to that statement. Is the statement fair? Is it true? If you don't think that there is clear evidence in the stories, think more generally about how the story might point you in the direction of a response to the statement.

(a) God gave Adam and Eve *real* freedom.

(b) God changed his mind.

(c) God knew everything that was going to happen in the story.

(d) God was fair to Adam and Eve.

(e) God over-reacted to Adam and Eve's choice.

(f) God should never have given them any choice in the first place.

2 Now read through the story of Job and create a visual display of the things that happened to him. For each of the things that happened think about the following:

■ Was this fair on Job?

■ Why might God have done this to Job?

■ Should God have done this to Job?

3 In the story of the escape of the Israelites from Egypt, God lends a hand to destroy the Egyptian army. Imagine you are the child of one of the Egyptian soldiers who has been killed. Write a letter to the Israelites' God expressing your views about what has happened and inviting the Israelites' God to explain to you why your dad has been killed by a God that he couldn't possibly have defeated.

4 Carry out an Internet search by asking the question: 'Was the God of the Old Testament cruel?' Present your findings to your class. What different views are held about this question? You could look at *The Skeptic's Annotated Bible*, which has highlighted Bible texts that it thinks shows God to be cruel. (See **www.skepticsannotatedbible. com/cruelty/short.html**)

5 Before you read the next sources, discuss in what ways you think Jesus' behaviour was different from the behaviour of God in the Old Testament.

Source 3

What did Jesus teach us about God?

'I am a Christian, and yes I have read the Old Testament, but my beliefs about God are based on Jesus, who was also God after all. The God of the Old Testament wasn't all hellfire and brimstone. Here's what I think Jesus teaches us about God or, rather, reminds us about God:

■ God cares for people; he sent Jesus to die for our sins.

■ God forgives people; Jesus even forgave those who killed him.

■ God wants to help people; Jesus cured the sick and made the lame walk.

■ God understands people; Jesus knew what it was like to be human, he even put up with children when he was tired!

■ God only gets angry with humans when they aren't all they can be; Jesus got annoyed with the traders in the temple.

■ God loves people; Jesus accepted everyone, no matter who they were, and he preached tolerance and respect.

I think Jesus wanted to show us God's soft side: that he wasn't the terrible tyrant of the past. Perhaps he was just putting right what the writers of the Bible had got wrong.'

Activity 2

1 In groups, choose one of the bullet points from Source 3 and prepare a short presentation on this for your class. Your presentation should include:

(a) an explanation of what is meant by the chosen statement (e.g. 'God cares for people')

(b) at least two points of evidence from the life of Jesus illustrating this statement

(c) an explanation of how this view of God is similar to and different from the God of the Old Testament.

You can present your research to your class as a talk or illustrated display, or in any way you like. You should be prepared to answer questions on your presentation.

2 Christians believe that Jesus was God in human form, so that he was actually God. What questions does this raise for Christians (and anyone else) in your group? Come up with as many questions as you can about any issues this might raise. Here's one example: 'If Jesus was God, then he knew everything. How could he have normal human relationships when he knew everything the person he was talking to was just about to say or do ...?'

Source 4

'As time went on of course, views of God changed. Some people seemed to prefer the mighty God of the Old Testament, while others seemed to prefer the softer God shown in the person of Jesus. Also, maybe some people saw God the way they wanted to see him. If they were fighting in a war, perhaps they wanted a powerful God who would help them in battle; if they were facing trouble in life perhaps they wanted a more compassionate God. Some people began to see God as more remote – a being outside of space and time that we could never really know – and that only the priesthood could communicate with. Others began to see him more in a personal way, involved in every aspect of their daily lives. For some, God felt further away than ever; for others, closer.'

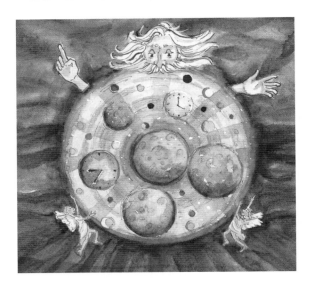

Source 5

Some statements about God:

(a) God punishes the wicked.

(b) God hates sinners.

(c) God helps those who help themselves.

(d) God is on our side.

(e) God answers prayers.

(f) God loves everyone equally.

(g) People only call on God when they need him.

(h) God forgives anything.

(i) God has no needs.

(j) There are some things God should apologise for.

(k) We can never really know God.

(l) God can be seen in the beauty of nature.

(m) God is not out there, he's in here.

(n) God cannot make mistakes.

(o) The universe will end, but God won't.

(p) God appears all the time ... in good people.

(q) God is the meaning of life.

(r) God has some important questions to answer.

Activity 3

1 It is said that God made humans in his image. Some say that humans make God in their image, or in the way that suits them best. What do you think? Discuss your responses to this statement and share your ideas.

2 Use the statements in Source 5 to create your own sticky note vote. Put a copy of each statement up in various places in your classroom and then write your own response, on a sticky note, to as many of the statements as you like. Then stick them under the statement. Once completed, take some time to walk around the room and reflect on other people's responses to each of the statements.

3 Link with history. Create your own timeline of views about God. You should include the following (very!) broad time periods: the Old Testament; the time of Jesus; the early Christian Church; the Middle Ages; the Enlightenment; the nineteenth and twentieth centuries; the twenty-first century. In what ways were people's views about God different in these times … and if they were, why?

2 Exploring the existence of God 2: contemporary views of God

Source 1

'As a Christian, I believe that God made us in his own image. This means that he looks like we do, and so, I suppose, he could look like anyone really. Perhaps the old man in the sky with the long white beard is how we think of him because that's an ancient idea of what a wise and kind person looks like – and I guess that's how we see God.'

Source 2

'As a Christian, I too believe that God made us in his own image. This means that we are like him, but it doesn't have to be in a physical way. Maybe we are just like him in our personalities or our personal qualities. Maybe it's just that we can think about the past, present and future in a way that no other living thing can. Maybe that's how we are like God.'

Activity 1

1 What questions would you ask the two Christians in Sources 1 and 2?

2 Take a sheet of A3 paper and consider some questions that people might have about the idea of God. Your questions should begin with 'What? Where? Why? When? How?' Display and discuss your questions.

3 For the moment, let's leave the question that asks whether or not there is a god. Here are some other questions about God that people often ask. How would you answer these? What other answers do you think might be given in answer to these? You can answer in any way you like, either in writing or in some other form.

- Does God live in a physical place?
- Is God spiritual or physical or some mixture of both?
- Does God have a physical body?
- What would God look like?
- Would God's appearance stay the same or change according to the situation?

- If God has a physical body, would he, for example, need to have his hair cut every now and then?
- If there's only one God, might he ever get lonely?
- Can God get things wrong?
- Does God get grumpy, angry, bored ...?

4 There are many great pieces of art that depict God. Find a variety of these online and explain how each one depicts God. What problems might a religious person have with God being depicted in this way? Why has the artist depicted God in this way?

Source 3

'God is just a fairy tale made up by people to explain what they don't understand. How anyone can believe in such a being in the modern world beats me. It's no different from believing in Santa or the tooth fairy. Grow up people, there is no God. God didn't make humans, humans made God.'

Source 4

'Now we've even got 'celebrity atheists' all over TV. They tell us that there is no God; they throw science at us like we know what they're talking about, and as if science proves that there's no God. They make snide remarks about religious people; in fact, they treat us as if we're just dull and ignorant. Well aren't they just as closed minded as some of the people they're continually slagging off?'

Activity 2

1 What does each of the sources above say about God? What do you think about what is being said? Do a 'think, pair, share' exercise. Think about your own views, and then share with another person, then share with another pair.

THERE'S PROBABLY NO GOD.
NOW STOP WORRYING AND ENJOY YOUR LIFE.

2 Are people who don't believe in God people with closed minds? Create a sticky note board in answer to this question.

3 Should anyone be allowed to say anything about anything, anywhere? Should people's religious beliefs be protected from criticism? Display the pros and cons of such an approach to responding to people's beliefs.

4 The poster above is from a recent campaign to challenge belief in God. Design your own poster that supports belief in God.

Source 5

In a recent earthquake, many thousands of innocent people were killed. The quake came without warning and devastated an already poor country. However, among the terrible stories of the dead were stories of little miracles too. People who survived against the odds. People who were presumed dead then turned up alive. People who managed to escape the quake because a strange chain of events meant that they were somewhere that the quake did little harm instead of where they should have been — right in the danger zone. The population of the country where the quake occurred is very strongly Christian and services of worship have been held to thank God for those who survived.

Damage from the earthquake in Haiti, 2010

Activity 3

1 Source 5 raises many issues for debate. Having read the source, discuss the possible questions it raises and how the idea of God can be supported or challenged by the events of the quake. Then choose a debate motion and propose and defend this motion.

2 One-minute challenge: You have a timed one minute to talk about what you have learned during your study of this topic. (If you want a bigger challenge, talk for more minutes!)

Source 1

Our Faither, yer up in the glory
Pure dead special is yer name
Let yer reign come on doon
Let whit you want be done
Doon here like up there
Gie us some nosh right noo (please)
And gie's a break for oor dodgy times
And let us cut others a wee bit o' slack tae
Steer us well away fae the stuff we know we
shouldny be daein
And shove us away fae the dark side
For everthin's yours, a' the clout and a' the credit
A' the time and a' oer the place
Amen tae that.

Source 2

I'm not a sheep, but the Lord is my Shepherd
I'm not exactly flush, but I want for nothing
He makes life good for me
He walks with me along the lonely riverside
He cheers me up like nothing else
He points me in the right way
So I don't show Him up
Even when the going gets tough
I can still look trouble in the eye
Because He's with me
Making me cosy
He builds me up
Even when others are knocking me down
I can't believe my luck sometimes
He'll always be there for me
And I'll always be there for Him.

Activity 1

1 Source 1 is a version of the Lord's Prayer, as told by Jesus as an example of how to pray. Carry out an Internet search into some different versions of this prayer in the Christian Bible. What are the similarities and differences? In a group, write your own version of this prayer taking a couple of lines each. You could write this in any style of language you like.

2 Source 2 is a version of Psalm 23. Read one or more versions of the original. Now use this psalm as the basis for a slide show where each image represents one of the lines of the psalm.

3 Christians think of the Bible as a library rather than a book. It contains many different styles of writing. Create your own class display showing the different styles of writing in the Bible (for example, poetry, history) and give an example of each style of writing as part of your display.

4 On the next page are some statements about the Bible that might be given by Christians. Everyone in your class will be given one of these statements. Your job is then to explain the statement and take any questions others in class have about it.

(a) The Bible was written by humans so may contain errors.

(b) The Bible was written by humans under God's instruction so contains no errors.

(c) The Bible was written in different times for different reasons.

(d) The Bible tells us all we need to know about life.

(e) You should obey what the Bible says at all times.

(f) The Bible is just a guidebook; you have to make sense of it for yourself.

(g) When trying to make sense of the Bible you have to use your brain.

(h) You should not try to understand the Bible, just follow it.

Source 3

'When I read the Bible, I obviously try to make sense of it for my own life. I don't think you have to be a professor at a university to be able to do that but, yes, sometimes it's hard to see what it's getting at. So, over the years I have developed a plan for understanding any Bible passage I read. I find it works for me, but you shouldn't always expect that it will make complete sense first time round! Here's my plan. What do you think?

1 Read the passage very carefully.

2 Step away from it and think about it for an hour or so.

3 Think about what it meant to the people who first heard it. Was it trying to tell them something specifically about their lives?

4 Think about any situation in the modern world that is similar to the Bible passage. Can I match up then and now?

5 Talk to other people about the Bible passage and get their views; two heads are better than one, after all.'

Activity 2

1 Look at some Bible passages. Before any discussion, write down what you think the message in the passage is. Then, in your group, follow the plan in Source 3 (make your hour five silent minutes!) and discuss each section of the plan in relation to your passage.

You can select your Bible passage by randomly opening a Bible and then randomly selecting a passage. The length of the passage you use will depend upon the style of writing it is.

2 Once you have completed this, think about how you could summarise the passage you have read as:

(a) a newspaper billboard

(b) the tag line for a movie

(c) a TV commercial

(d) a tweet.

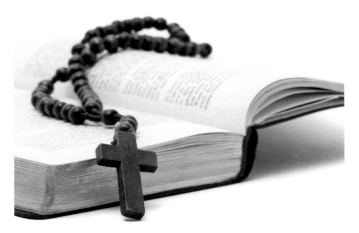

A printed copy of the Bible

Source 4

- The Bible can say anything you want it to say.
- The Bible is just the story book of people in the past.
- The Bible shows us what God is really like.
- The Bible is God showing us who he is in a way that makes sense to us.
- The Bible contains useful parts and useless ones.
- No one reads the Bible any more.
- The Bible is a helpful guide in a confusing world.
- The Bible can comfort those in need.
- The Bible reminds us of who we are and, more importantly, who we could be.
- The Bible is the best way to make sense of life.

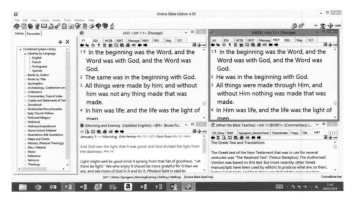

Another version of the Bible

Source 5

'I don't just read the Bible and get my understanding of God from what I read; it's just one part of the way God makes himself known to me. I pray and I get guidance that way too. Not a voice from the sky, but just knowing that my prayer has been listened to and answered. I see God in the actions of others, I see him in the beauty of nature. I hear him in music, I feel him in the care and love shown by others for the world in which they live. The Bible isn't some book written to prove that there is a god, it's just one of the ways in which God points out to us who he is and why he matters.'

Activity 3

1 For each of the statements in Source 4, decide whether you agree, disagree or don't know about it. Do this on your own, and then compare responses across your class. You should do this anonymously as you might get a better picture of what people really believe. What does your class think of the Bible?

2 The Gideons organisation distributes Bibles for free in schools as well as giving them to many hotels, which often put one in each room. Why do you think they do this? Do you think it is a good idea? What benefits do they think it brings?

3 In Source 5, the person thinks that she sees God in the world in many different ways, not just through the Bible. For each of the ways she has described, think about what this might mean for her in practice. Also, think about how someone might give a different explanation for what she thinks is evidence of God.

Source 1

The 99 names of Allah

All-Merciful; All-Beneficent; Ruler; Pure; Source of Peace; Inspirer of Faith; Guardian; Victorious; Compeller; Greatest; Creator; Maker of Order; Shaper of Beauty; Forgiving; Subduer; Giver; Sustainer; Opener; Knower; Constrictor; Reliever; Abaser; The Exalter; Bestower of Honours; Humiliator; Hearer; Seer; Judge; Just; Subtle; All-Aware; Forbearing; Magnificent; Forgiver and Hider of Faults; Rewarder of Thankfulness; Highest; Greatest; Preserver; Nourisher; Accounter; Mighty; Generous; Watchful; Responder to Prayer; All-Comprehending; Perfectly Wise; Loving; Majestic; Resurrector; Witness; Truth; Trustee; Possessor of All Strength; Forceful; Governor; Praised; Appraiser; Originator; Restorer; Giver of Life; Taker of Life; Ever Living; Self-Existing; Finder; Glorious; Only One; One; Satisfier of All Needs; All Powerful; Creator of All Power; Expediter; Delayer; First; Last; Manifest; Hidden; Protecting Friend; Supreme; Doer of Good; Guide to Repentance; Avenger; Forgiver; Clement; Owner of All; Lord of Majesty and Bounty; Equitable; Gatherer; Rich; Enricher; Preventer of Harm; Creator of The Harmful; Creator of Good; Light; Guide; Originator; Everlasting; Inheritor; Righteous Teacher; Patient

Abridged from www.sufism.org/foundations/ninety-nine-names/the-most-beautiful-names-of-allah-2

Arabic calligraphy

Source 2

'As a Muslim, how do I find out about what Allah wants? First there is the Qur'an: the actual words of Allah. This is the first and most important source. Then the Hadith: these are the reported sayings and teachings of Muhammad, our prophet; they even include rules about when you can't eat garlic! Then there is the Sharia: this is the law. Finally, there are the Qiyas: these are what we call analogies, and they try to cover things that do not appear obviously in the Qur'an. For example, when coffee was discovered, Muslims had to decide if it was OK to drink it or not. The Qur'an doesn't mention coffee, so the Qiyas are ways that Muslim teachers have tried to work out if coffee is like anything in the Qur'an, then they made their decision about it.'

A copy of the Qur'an

Activity 1

1 Look at the 99 names of Allah. In groups, discuss the following and report your thoughts to the class:

   (a) Are there any names there that surprise you?
   (b) Are there any names that you don't understand?
   (c) Which names appear more than once and why do you think they do?
   (d) Which names appear also to have their opposites in the list?
   (e) What do you think this list of names tells us about what Muslims think Allah is like?

2   Choose three of the 99 names. For each one, explain what you think this might mean in practice and how this name might affect the way a Muslim lives his or her life. Here's an example:

Watchful: I think this means that Allah keeps an eye on everything. For a Muslim, this means that she or he should remember that whatever they do, Allah will see it. I think this would make you live your life more carefully.

3   For Muslims, the Qur'an is the final source on how to live your life, but the Hadith also helps with day-to-day decisions. Try an Internet search on 'Hadith and X'. Replace X with something you'd like to know about and see if there are any teachings in the Hadith about this.

4   The Qiyas try to help Muslims respond to modern life. In your group, come up with a list of questions that you think might not have been written about in the Qur'an or the Hadith. For example: Should someone have the right to sell their organs for transplant?

5   Most Muslim countries base their laws on Sharia law. What kinds of things do you think Sharia law will cover? How might it be different in different Muslim countries? What similarities might there be between Sharia law and the law in Scotland?

Source 3

Who and what is Allah?

Some Muslims give their own views about Allah's most important qualities:

■   'I see Allah as power. He is the creator of the universe and keeps everything in it going. He's concerned with the big picture, but also with the tiny details. You can't imagine his power, it's way beyond our understanding.'

■   'I see Allah as more personal, a being who is involved in every aspect of your daily life. Of course he's all-powerful, but I think too that he concerns himself with me and all that I do.'

■   'When I was younger, I was a little frightened of Allah. I was afraid that he was looking at me all the time and judging me. I was too young at that time to really understand that he looks at my life with compassion. Yes, I still believe that he will judge me, but I think he wants to guide me first, so that when it comes to judgement, I'll have done the right thing. So I concentrate more on his kindness now than his judgement.'

■   'I agree that there are two sides to Allah: there is the all-powerful, mighty being and the more personal, forgiving one. For everything about Allah that appears forbidding, there is another aspect that is understanding and forgiving. Allah has shown himself in the Qur'an. So, to understand him properly, we must read it … and live by it.'

Activity 2

1   In Islam, it is forbidden to create any image of Allah or the prophet Muhammad. Why do you think this is? In some other religions, such as Christianity, paintings and images of God and Jesus are quite common, even in religious buildings. Why do you think there are differences between these two religions on this point? Has one got it right and the other wrong?

2   From your study and research in this section, how would you answer the following questions?
   (a) What view of Allah do Muslims have?
   (b) How does belief in Allah affect the lives of individual Muslims?

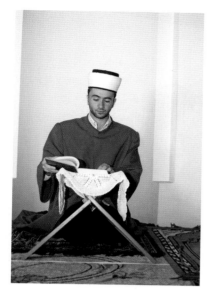

A man reading the Qur'an

'I was on holiday in Dubai, and everywhere I heard people saying: 'Insha'Allah'. They'd say it at the end of a sentence, sometimes even after something as simple as: 'When I get home from my work today.' They told me it means 'God willing' and is about the Muslim belief that everything is in Allah's hands. It doesn't mean you're not free to make your own decisions, it just means that everything you do depends upon Allah wanting it to be so. It's not him controlling you: one man said that it reminds him that Allah guides him, and that if Allah wants this for him then it will happen. That comforted him — and that can't be bad.'

Children studying the Qur'an

A mosque in Dubai

'Yes, I do pray five times a day, and no, it's not a hassle. It helps me in my daily life; it helps me make sense of the world; it helps me get closer to Allah; and it helps me understand myself better too. There are formal prayers called Salah. These are set and very structured; but there are also the dua prayers. Basically this means calling out to Allah whenever you need to — and it can be about anything at all — from saying thank you for a nice day, to asking for a bit of help with a job interview. You can do du'a prayer anytime. Prayer helps keep my feet on the ground; it's good to know that Allah is always there for you.'

Activity 3

1 Create your own display of the different kinds of prayer that are carried out in Islam. Distinguish between the Salah and dua prayers.

2 Keep a reflection diary for a few days. What things might you offer up a dua prayer for (or did if you are Muslim)? How many times did you think about this and what kinds of things would you have prayed for? Think also about what you have learned about the nature of Allah. Would Allah have responded to your dua prayer?

3 In groups, draw up a list of arguments for and against the following statement: 'You can only do what Allah wants for you.'

Source 1

'As a Hindu, how would I explain God? Now that's a tricky one. First off, he is part of everything and apart from everything. He is unknowable and yet he responds to us personally. I'm saying he, but I could just as well say she, or 'it' even. God is Brahman and Brahman is all that there is. One great Hindu teacher said that Brahman can be described by saying that he's not this and not that … but that's not helping you get a picture is it? Brahman is formless, but he can choose to take on a form – any kind of form, human, animal, plant – whatever. We do have names for Brahman's forms which help us to make sense of him better. We think of him as Brahma the creator, Vishnu the preserver and Shiva the destroyer. These are just names though, ways in which Brahman acts and ways to explain what he does. There are also many other avatars of Brahman … too many to name.'

Vishnu

Brahman

Shiva

'OK, I won't name them all, there are many, but I'll try to explain something about it. To help us relate to Brahman, and to teach us certain things, Brahman, as Vishnu, has taken on forms throughout the history of the universe. Each form has a different story and a different message, and helps us to know something about the unknowable Brahman.

There's Rama, a great hero in Hindu stories; he teaches us about loyalty, devotion, courage and so on. There's Krishna, another human form who has much to teach us. There's Matsya too, a fish who rescued the Holy Scriptures and reminds us of the importance of our holy teachings. These aren't really gods; they're representations of Brahman – ways of making sense of him/her/it.'

Activity 1

1 Use the information in Sources 1 and 2 to discuss and answer the following questions:
   (a) Do Hindus believe in one God or many gods, or both one God and many gods?
   (b) 'Brahman is not this and not that.' What is helpful and unhelpful about describing Brahman in this way?

2 It is common for Hindus to choose which aspect of Brahman and which avatars they worship. For example, a learner might worship Ganesh, who is linked with learning. Think about the most important features of your life, the things that matter to you. What kind of aspect of Brahman would you choose to worship? If you visit **www.hindunet.org/god/summary/index.htm** you'll find a list of gods here, and you might find one that matches the things that are important in your life. Alternatively type 'list of Hindu gods' into any search engine and see what you find.

3 Hindus believe that every individual is responsible for their relationship with Brahman. In groups, think about the possible advantages and disadvantages of this approach to faith. Write these on cards and then give them to another group to sort into advantages and disadvantages.

4 Consider Brahma, Vishnu and Shiva and create a short presentation on each in a style of your choice. You should show how each aspect links to the other two.

5 Avatars of Vishnu teach us important things or show qualities we should aim for. In your group, list the kinds of qualities you think are necessary for a happy and purposeful life. Alternatively, what do you think are the most important messages that any god could communicate to humans?

Source 3

Krishna and the milkmaids

One avatar of Vishnu, called Krishna, was sometimes a naughty child and later as a young man, was happy to play tricks on people. One day, he and some friends arrived at a bathing spot to find some milkmaids bathing in the water. (Some of the stories say he followed the milkmaids to the river.) When the milkmaids got to the river they removed their clothes and went bathing. Krishna appeared from behind the bushes and took their clothes. He then teased the girls before eventually giving them back their clothes – though some stories say not until they were out of the water!

Krishna and the milkmaids

Activity 2

1 The story in Source 3 (on page 15) is a popular one among Hindus, but you might be wondering what it has to say about the nature of Vishnu and Brahman! Here are some possible explanations, though you might disagree with some. Put these in order, from the explanation you think most likely to the one you think least likely. If you want to include your own explanation, feel free to add it. There is no right or wrong answer here.

   (a) The story shows that Brahman appreciates what it means to be human.
   (b) The story reminds us that religious stories can be about everyday events.
   (c) The story is understood by many Hindus as playful, so humour and play must be important to Brahman.
   (d) The story is an example of how not to treat people.
   (e) The story is symbolic of the relationship between humans and Brahman.
   (f) The story gets us thinking about the difference between teasing and bullying.
   (g) The meaning of the story is what you make it; it's just to get you thinking.

2 There are many other stories of Krishna, which at first will seem a little strange if you do not have a Hindu background. Find an example of another story of Krishna and, in groups, prepare a short presentation on this story which should include:

   ■ a re-telling of the story
   ■ some possible explanations of the meaning of the story
   ■ what your group thinks a Hindu would believe about the story (or does believe if any of you are Hindu).

   You can find many stories of Krishna on the Internet, for example at **www.4to40.com/story/ default.asp?k=Krishna**.

Source 4

'Do I worship statues? Well yes and no is the answer to that really. I don't worship the object itself, although of course Brahman is in everything, so anything could really be an object of worship I suppose. In practice, we worship a murti; this is a very particular image of an aspect of Brahman. Sometimes the image is a statue, or just a picture. Sometimes the image involves symbolic things like Shiva dancing and standing on ignorance, for example. Sometimes it's like Ganesh and his elephant's head, which reminds us of a story. The image itself is just a way to get closer to Brahman and a way to make solid something that is formless. We treat our images with care but then, as they represent the life-force of everything that exists, so we should. Which image you worship is up to you.'

Ganesh

'In puja, or worship, we make contact with Brahman. It gives us a focus for our prayers. It just makes it easier to worship when you have something solid in front of you rather than thinking about Brahman, which is just an abstract idea. It also adds some colour and interest to our worship. In fact, I think puja appeals to all of our senses, and that's a good thing. I think if you approach God with all your senses in use, the experience will be more real and more meaningful to you. So, it might all look a bit strange to you, but for us it helps us to make contact with the energy of life all around us, and that helps in so many ways.'

Activity 3

1 Find an example of a Hindu god statue or image. Create a display that informs people in your class about the symbolism used in the image. You should aim to show what this image communicates to the Hindu about the nature of Brahman, or what messages it communicates to Hindus. Perhaps you could take your exhibition to your nearest primary school.

2 Watch a video of a Hindu puja. How does it appeal to all five senses?

3 Just as in other religions, Hindus will ask certain things of God. What kinds of things might they ask for? Which of these do you think would be appropriate to ask of God? Here's one example to get you thinking: A Hindu athlete asks Brahman to help him win in his sport.

A Hindu family carrying out puja

6 The cosmological argument: religious responses

Source 1

The classic cosmological argument

1 Everything that exists must have a cause.
2 The universe obviously exists.
3 So there must be a cause for the universe.
4 That cause could only be God.
5 Therefore God must exist.

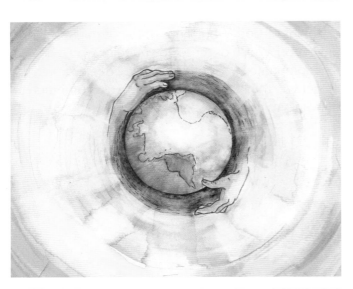

Source 2

The kalam cosmological argument

1 Everything that begins in time must have a cause.
2 The universe began in time.
3 So there must have been a cause for the universe.
4 That cause could only be God.
5 Therefore God must exist.

Activity 1

1 In groups of four, take each of the different cosmological arguments set out in Sources 1 and 2. For each argument, two of you should defend the argument while the other two question and challenge it. Then swap and debate the other argument. Does one pair have an easier task? Why might this be?

2 Now, in your group, take both of the cosmological arguments and for each line, think of as many questions as you can in response. What kinds of question does it raise? How do you think a religious person (from any of the three religions you have looked at so far, for example) might respond to it?

3 The cosmological arguments are linked to the following historical figures: Plato, Aristotle, Aquinas and Al-Ghazali (among others). Choose one of these figures and carry out some research into his life and teachings. What do you think motivated him to use the cosmological argument as a way of proving the existence of God? Present your findings and your views to your class.

4 What views do people in your class or school have about this argument? Carry out some research by reading either of the two arguments to people who are *not* studying RMPS. Then ask them to rate, on a scale of 1 to 10, how well they think this proves the existence of God (1 = doesn't prove it at all and 10 = completely proves it). Display your findings in class in graphical form with written summaries of what you think your results are telling you.

5 As a group, can you think of any way to improve the cosmological argument so that it does a better job of proving the existence of God?

Source 3

'As a Christian and a scientist, I'm afraid I don't find philosophy of much use these days. I mean, the idea of just sitting and thinking isn't going to bring solutions, only research and evidence does that. That's why I think science has now replaced philosophy. Although I do think the kalam cosmological argument is quite good – but for scientific reasons, not philosophical ones. The problem with the classic cosmological argument was that scientists in the past thought the universe had always existed. The Big Bang theory shows that's not true. The universe did have a beginning in time. That means that I can believe in a God who is outside of time who started the universe off. I know that's still a belief, but it's one that you can't prove or disprove … so I'm sticking with it for a whole load of other reasons!'

Christians at worship

Activity 2

1 Play your own version of the TV programme *Mastermind*, with your RMPS teacher and a science teacher as the contestants. Their specialist subject should be: The Big Bang and the cosmological argument. After some research, devise a list of questions for them. Perhaps after you've put them through this, they'll do it to you!

2 Here are some statements about the relationship between 'proving the existence of God' and science. For each one, discuss what you think it means and offer your own views about it:

(a) God can never be proved by science.

(b) God could be a hypothesis supported by science.

(c) Science involves just as much faith as religion.

(d) Even if science had evidence for God, we would not recognise the evidence.

(e) The universe *is* evidence for the existence of God.

(f) God would not want there to be scientific evidence for his existence.

3 Source 3 said that he was sticking with his faith 'for a whole load of other reasons'. Based on what you have learned about Christianity, what might these reasons be? Who can come up with most?

Source 4

My faith has found a resting place
Not in device nor creed;
I trust the Ever-living One
His wounds for me shall plead.

I need no other argument
I need no other plea;
It is enough that Jesus died,
And that He died for me.
 Eliza E. Hewitt, in *Songs of Joy and Gladness*, 1891

Source 5

I am not skilled to understand
What God hath willed, what God hath planned;
I only know that at His right hand
Is One Who is my Saviour!

I take Him at His word indeed;
'Christ died for sinners' – this I read;
For in my heart I find a need
Of Him to be my Saviour!
 Dorothy Greenwell, *Songs of Salvation*, 1873

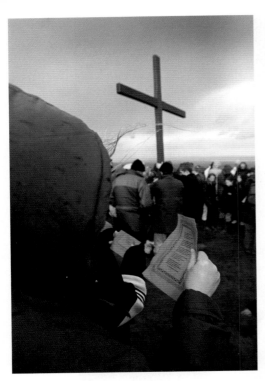

Christians at worship

Activity 3

1 Split your class into two. Each side should take one of the hymns in Sources 4 and 5 (on page 19). You should prepare an explanation for this hymn and try to answer the following questions:

(a) What is its message?

(b) What might have led to the writer creating it?

(c) Would all Christians agree with it?

(d) What might the scientist in Source 3 (on page 19) think about it?

(e) Does the meaning of this hymn support or reject the cosmological argument?

(f) The hymns clearly stress the importance of faith as opposed to reason. In what way do they do this?

2 In Christianity, as in other religions, there is sometimes disagreement between those who think that all you need is faith, and those who think you should also use reason to work out the truth of your beliefs. Is accepting, or rejecting, the cosmological argument an example of faith, reason or a mixture of the two? Discuss this in your class and note any views expressed.

3 Is it possible that studying arguments like the cosmological argument is just something you do in RMPS and something that ordinary religious people don't really think much about? Carry out some research with followers of a faith in your own community. Find out how much they know about the cosmological argument and what they think about it. You could display your findings in their religious building if they will let you.

Source 1

'Philosophically, the cosmological argument just doesn't work and here's why:

1 Why does everything need a cause? That's just based on observation and experience. If we based everything on what we see and experience then we'd still think the Earth was flat! Maybe the universe didn't need to be caused at all.

2 Even if the universe did need to be caused, you can't just jump from that to deciding that it must have been caused by any god we recognise in our world's religions. It could have been caused by a quite different god, or a group of gods; it could just as well have been a purple fairy.

3 OK, so let's say that we agree that the universe needed a cause – and then we answer that by saying that this cause was God, who didn't need to be caused. That's just silly. You might as well decide that the universe itself needed no cause if you're going to accept that God didn't need a cause; I mean … seriously?

4 The kalam argument doesn't do any better. Here, you have to accept that God is outside of time and space; so where and when is he? Also, if you accept that God didn't need a beginning in time, then why not just accept that the universe didn't either?

Give up guys, you're just contradicting yourselves.'

Source 2

'Scientifically, the cosmological argument doesn't work and here's why:

1 It is not based on evidence, just thinking, and that's not enough these days I'm afraid.

2 We think that at the Big Bang, time and space itself began, so there was no space for God to exist outside of, and no time before the Big Bang for him to exist.

3 The mysterious world of quantum physics is beginning to question the idea that everything needs a cause.

4 To say that the only possible cause of the universe is God is based on no evidence at all, unless you count wishful thinking as evidence.

No, scientifically, saying that God caused the universe causes more problems than it solves.'

Activity 1

1 In groups of four, take each of the responses to the cosmological argument in Sources 1 and 2 (on page 21). Two of you should defend one of the responses and two should question and challenge it. Then swap roles (defenders become challengers and vice versa) and discuss the other response. Does one of the pairs have an easier task? Why might this be?

2 What is the difference between thought experiments and scientific experiments? Has philosophy been replaced by science? Discuss these questions and present your conclusions. If you have a philosophy teacher in your school perhaps she or he could defend philosophy!

3 'There are questions that science can answer and those that it can't.' Draw up a list of possible questions that support or reject this statement. For example, 'All swans are white' cannot be answered by science, because it could never gather all the evidence.

4 Carry out some research into the Big Bang and quantum physics (prepare to be boggled!). Present your findings in your own style. How far does each of these theories support or reject the idea that God was the first cause of everything?

5 The scientist Stephen Jay Gould said that the solution to the 'battle' between science and religion was that they should stick to what they do best and not try to do each other's job. (He called it non-overlapping magisteria.) In your group, discuss 'What does science do best?' and 'What does religion do best?' Should they try to keep apart, or try to match up their ways together?

Source 3

David Hume (1711–1776) was a philosopher who rejected the cosmological argument a long time ago. He agreed that things we observe in everyday life needed a cause, but he thought that to say this proved the whole universe needed a cause was a step too far.

Immanuel Kant (1724–1804) also disagreed with the cosmological argument. He said that being outside of space and time was just too difficult to get our heads around – and so any belief about such a being was just that, belief. So you could equally well believe in an uncaused universe as believe in a being outside of space and time.

David Hume

Immanuel Kant

Activity 2

1 Reciprocal reading: In pairs, choose either Kant or Hume. Read through the relevant part of Source 3, then teach the other person in your pair Kant or Hume's views about the cosmological argument. You could extend this activity by doing some further research on Kant or Hume.

2 The philosopher Bertrand Russell (1872–1970) said that because individual things need a cause doesn't mean everything does. In fact he said that just because every person has a mother doesn't mean there has to have been a first mother of all. What questions would you ask Russell, or what criticisms of his argument might there be?

3 What kinds of cause-and-effect do you notice in everyday life? Create a graffiti wall about this. Can things have more than one cause?

Bertrand Russell

Source 4

'As a Humanist, I'm still surprised that there are people who believe in the cosmological argument. Thinking up a God to explain how the universe began makes the problem more complicated, not less. For example, who made God? Is God subject to the laws of physics? How can anything be outside of space; where could that be? How can anything be outside of time; when would that be? If there was a God outside of space and time, then how can "he" have anything to do with anything that lives in space and time? Does he break through from space and time every now and again when needed? Religious people often say that God is close to them; how can he be close to everything, always, and yet still remain outside of space and time all the "time"? Can God break his own rules? The list of questions is endless and, of course, there's no way ever to prove or disprove them, so why live life based on a fantasy? Live it based on reality: observable, testable and predictable reality makes much more sense than God.'

Source 5

'I wouldn't call myself a Humanist, more an agnostic. You see, because no one can prove that there was a first cause for the universe, or disprove it, I prefer just to think that it's an unanswerable question and leave it at that. All these people who argue about it all the time, just what exactly are they arguing about? You can't decide one way or another, so just let people think what they want and leave it at that. It seems to be quite trendy at the moment to knock religion down, and don't get me wrong, it does have its faults, but live and let live I say. If you want to believe the universe started itself off, or it was created by a being who looks just like your Uncle Bob, then that's up to you.'

THERE'S PROBABLY NO GOD.
NOW STOP WORRYING AND ENJOY YOUR LIFE.

www.humanism.org.uk
www.richarddawkins.net
www.atheistcampaign.org

Activity 3

1 As a class, walk around the room with music playing in the background. Every time the music stops, get the person who has stopped nearest to you to answer your question, and explain why they think this. You should get your teacher to give each person one of the questions below:

(a) What do you know about Humanism?

(b) Does suggesting that a God made the universe make understanding the beginning of the universe more or less complicated?

(c) If God made the universe, who could have made God?

(d) Can anything be outside of space?

(e) Can anything be outside of time?

(f) What evidence do people give to support their belief that God is close to them?

(g) Could God break his own rules?

(h) Is believing in God just wishful thinking?

(i) What is an agnostic?

(j) Is there any point in discussing how the universe began?

(k) What difference does it make to anyone alive today if the universe began one way instead of another?

2 Humanists would argue that although there's no evidence to disprove the existence of God, it is not reasonable to believe in God. Some go further and would say that there are very good reasons why believing in God makes no sense. What do you think they might mean?

3 Use what you have learned in this chapter and in Chapter 6. Write out a series of statements about the cosmological argument and the existence of God on individual cards, and then sort these out according to whether you think they would be said by a Humanist or a religious person.

Source 1

'How can anyone look at the universe or even a leaf from a tree and not say that God must have created it? How could something so complicated, so beautiful and so powerful ever have come into being by chance? That just wouldn't make sense. They talk about the Goldilocks effect – that the Earth is perfectly positioned in the solar system for life to exist – and they make it sound like a fairy story, which it isn't. The only explanation is that God must have made it that way, and for a reason. They talk about the millions of years it has taken for life to get to where it is now – and they say that such a long time means that life is just a series of accidents, weird chance events. Well, I don't see how that can be. Even if you had an eternity, something as complicated as a human brain can't just have come together randomly. No, there has to be a guiding hand behind it all – and the only hand with the power to be that guide is God. Simple really.'

The intricacies of a leaf

Source 2

'William Paley came up with an argument way back in 1802 which for him proved there must be a God. He said: Imagine you were walking across a field one day and you came across a watch. Now, imagine thinking "Blimey, what an amazing act of chance, all those little cogs and wheels and springs, randomly assembling themselves into a watch without any help from any watchmaker. Who would have thought?" Of course, that's beyond daft. That couldn't happen, no matter how many billions of years you had. So, the only reasonable explanation is that something must have made that watch. Now, the universe is much more complicated than a watch, so could it too have randomly assembled itself from what was lying around? Of course not. The only sensible explanation is that something made it – and that could only be God.'

The cogs and wheels in a watch

Activity 1

1   Set up a speed-dating scenario in your class. Have four or six people each reading one of Sources 1 and 2 above. Now you should move around each person in turn and listen to their explanation of the source. You can ask them questions about their viewpoint if you like.

2   What examples are there in nature of 'beauty'? Does everyone agree that the same things are beautiful? What explains differences in opinion? You could create a display entitled 'Beauty in nature' then get people in your class to add sticky notes giving each item a beauty mark out of 10.

3   Carry out some further research into the Goldilocks effect. What does this say about life on Earth and the Earth itself? Why might a religious person see this as evidence for the existence of God? Why might someone disagree? Discuss your findings in class.

4   Look up 'The infinite monkey theorem' on the Internet. How does this link up with the Goldilocks effect? What do you think of this argument?

5   Create your own ABC of Paley's watchmaker argument (see page 25). For example, A is for 'Ah! I've stubbed my toe on a watch ...'

Beauty in nature

Cruelty in nature

'Now look around you. What *do* you see? You see a world where everything fits with everything else: everything is ordered, structured, perfect for the job it has to do. For everything in nature there is a place, and even the simplest living thing is incredibly complex and well structured. Now, are you really telling me that this happened by chance? Can you really believe that things just came to be out of nothing? Are you really saying that the order and structure of our incredible world is nothing more than a lucky accident? Come on. Look, I could lay out everything that is needed to build a jumbo jet on the ground, but I don't think that even if I could sit around watching it for a few billion years all of those parts would just spontaneously organise themselves into a functioning jumbo jet. There must have been a guiding hand behind it all, and that could only have been God.'

Activity 2

1   The constant theme in religious responses to the teleological argument is that 'everything could only have been created by God'. What other possibilities are there? Use sticky notes to create a display of people's views about this. What else could have designed a universe?

2   The design argument is based on the idea that the universe is well designed for its purpose. Can you think of any examples in nature that look as though they are not well designed? Sit in a circle in class. Each student should offer one possible idea about this. You can pass if you like.

3   Imagine you were designing a whole new world. What would this world be like? In what ways would it be similar to or different from Earth as it is now?

Activity 3

1 You have been asked to write some more verses of the hymn in Source 4 in the same style. As a group, write the verses; you could perhaps take a line each. What other things in the natural world would Christians want to recognise and celebrate?

2 Carry out your own research and display your findings. You should ask a variety of people if they think the universe (or life itself!) has a purpose, and if so what is it? What views are held? How do different age groups answer these questions? What do people's answers tell you about their beliefs?

3 Some Christians believe that the design argument isn't just a philosophical idea, but has scientific support. They call themselves 'Creationists' and/ or 'Creation scientists'. Carry out some Internet research about these viewpoints. What do they claim? How do others challenge their claims?

Source 4

All things bright and beautiful,
All creatures great and small,
All things wise and wonderful,
The Lord God made them all.

Each little flower that opens,
Each little bird that sings,
He made their glowing colours,
He made their tiny wings.

The purple-headed mountain,
The river running by,
The sunset and the morning,
That brightens up the sky.

The cold wind in the winter,
The pleasant summer sun,
The ripe fruits in the garden,
He made them every one.

The tall trees in the greenwood,
The meadows for our play,
The rushes by the water,
To gather every day.

He gave us eyes to see them,
And lips that we might tell
How great is God Almighty,
Who has made all things well.

Cecil Frances Alexander, All Things Bright and Beautiful, 1850

Source 5

The teleological argument says that the universe was designed for a purpose. What might that purpose be? Some religious people suggest:

'The purpose is to praise God and to show his power and might.'

'The purpose is to provide the conditions necessary for life.'

'The purpose is a mystery; it's enough that God knows what it is.'

'The purpose will be revealed to us when God thinks we need to know it.'

'The purpose isn't our business; it's God's alone.'

'I don't worry too much about purpose, I just enjoy the world that God has made for us.'

The teleological argument: philosophical responses

Source 1

'Design?! I'll give you design! If this is the best the almighty can come up with, then it hardly shows him in a good light, does it? Let's face it, nature isn't beautiful and sweet-natured; it's harsh, brutal and violent. Look again at that pretty scene of little seedlings striving towards the sunlight. They're under attack from insects, bacteria and a careless footstep as you wander through them. They even try to crowd each other out so the strongest win: if God made them it seems that he favours only the strong. Don't forget too that as you bask in the warm sunlight, it's a massive thermonuclear reactor whose energy is based on violence. And then there's randomness: stray comets and meteors hurtling around the universe, ready to pulverise Earth at any time. Some designer!'

Source 2

'OK, apart from the fact that the universe isn't all that well designed, just because something appears designed doesn't mean that it is. And even if it was designed by something that doesn't mean that it has to have been a God, and certainly not any God who is believed in today. So Paley found a watch and assumed that it couldn't have been around there forever; why not? What if it had been a pile of stones instead of a watch? And, anyway, a watch is a bad example. David Hume said that the universe is more like a living thing than a watch; watches are obviously made, living things aren't, they reproduce and develop over many millions of years so that when you meet the end result you don't need to imagine any designer behind it other than chance. Besides, if a God designed the universe, who designed that God? If you believe in God you just shift the problem of design from the universe to God! If people want to believe in God, let them, but let's not pretend that the universe is anything other than evidence for the existence of the universe!'

Activity 1

1 Throughout the history of the Earth there have been a number of times when mass extinctions have occurred. This is where huge numbers of living things have died out, never to return. Find out about one or more of these and discuss how such mass extinctions affect the teleological argument.

2 Look again at Paley's watchmaker argument (see Chapter 8, Source 2 on page 25) and imagine that this time, instead of coming across a watch in a field, Paley comes across some stones, neatly stacked one on top of the other. Write an imaginative account of what might be going through Paley's mind. Would he still conclude that an intelligent designer must have made this?

3 A snowflake is perfectly and beautifully structured. Does this show that each one was designed by God?

4 Comets, meteors and the like seem to suggest a pretty random universe. We know that there are even galaxies in the universe that are crashing into each other with unbelievable destructive force. Is the universe just a series of random events? Does this randomness question the existence of an intelligent designer?

5 Find out more about David Hume's objections to the teleological argument. Design a short magazine article about this.

Source 3

'Richard Dawkins uses the existence of the eye to reject the teleological argument. He points out that if we look at an eye, then we see that it is incredibly good at what it does — so good, in fact, that we could easily assume that it has been designed for its purpose. However, the only "designer" is the millions of years of natural selection, which is evolution. "Eyes" probably started off as single cells that developed a sensitivity to changes in light: over millions of years, nature selected chance mutations to these "eyes" so that each helpful change brought greater advantage to the creature that had it, meaning that it was better able to survive and so reproduce — and pass on the benefits of its improved "eye". So, our incredibly complex human eyes (and others in nature that are even better than ours!) are the end result of evolutionary change, not intelligent design. They might appear designed, but they aren't.'

Eyes exist in a variety of forms

Activity 2

1 Create a display about the eye. You could look at a range of different eyes in nature and plot how these might have evolved over time. How do they fit with the teleological argument? You could point out that some eyes 'appear designed' to help their owners hunt and kill more effectively. If God designed those, then what does that say about God?

2 Dawkins also suggests that if there is life anywhere else in the universe then it too might have 'eyes', but that these eyes will have developed according to the conditions on the planet on which that life exists. Imagine a range of different conditions on another planet and suggest how eyes might have evolved to cope with that (for example, a planet with only two per cent of the sunlight that we have here on Earth).

3 The arguments in this chapter suggest that the design of the universe could have been better. In your group, discuss how the design of the universe, and life in it, could be improved.

Source 4

'The teleological argument is about purpose, but any purpose in the universe seems to be a little confused and here's why:

- First off, the dinosaurs. These mighty creatures lived for a very long time on our planet, and then, one day, without reason or warning, a random piece of space rock hit the Earth and that was the end of the dinosaurs, never to return. So what was their purpose?
- Then there's our Sun. It might be glowing brightly today, but at some point in the future it will run out of energy and die, and life in our solar system will be no more. So what was its purpose?
- Next, other stars and galaxies in our universe are being born and dying all the time. Why this constant need for change? Do any of these dying stars have life around them which is now being randomly wiped out? What is the purpose?
- Last of all, some scientists think that our whole universe will one day cease to exist. Why? What was it all for?'

Source 5

'Let's not get depressed about the randomness of the universe. There's nothing we can do about it. What we can do is celebrate the beauty of the universe: its magic, elegance and power. We can marvel at its size and complexity, its structure and its order. We can peer down the microscope at microscopic life and feel a sense of wonder at its complexity and organisation. We can find that life clings to the most inhospitable conditions on our planet and moves on through the workings of evolution. We can stare deep into our universe and uncover the secrets of its very beginning. We can explore sub-atomic particles, learn about the natural world and our place in it. That's the magic of reality. We don't need to make up a God to fill it; it's amazing enough as it is.'

Activity 3

1 In Chapter 8, you read a Christian hymn about the natural world, 'All Things Bright and Beautiful'. Write your own song or poem that expresses the magic of reality without the need for any designer. Alternatively you could create a slide show or a PowerPoint®.

2 Does anything really need to have a purpose? Would your life change in any way if you thought there was no ultimate purpose for it all? Discuss your views in class.

3 Devise a courtroom drama where God is accused of designing a flawed universe. Make sure you have 'witnesses' for both sides.

Source 1

'You only have to switch on the news to know that something's not right with our world. It's nothing but murders, violence, poverty and general misery for humans everywhere – not to mention the horrors we inflict on animals, and which they carry out on each other of course. And even if it's not living things doing nasty things, nature itself is unpredictable and pretty evil most of the time: hurricanes, earthquakes, floods, droughts, disease. And that's all before we get to the fact that life just seems to be a series of lucky – or unlucky – accidents. You're just in the wrong place at the wrong time. It doesn't matter how well you have lived your life, how kind and loving you have been; none of that matters when some random act of cruelty or some unforeseen natural disaster ends up on your doorstep. And it's always been that way: unpredictable, uncontrolled, random and horrid. And all of this is meant to be looked over by a loving God?'

Poverty in a modern city

Source 2

'So here's the problem in as few words as possible. If you can do it in fewer then good luck to you!
1   Evil exists.
2   God doesn't stop it.
3   If he doesn't want to, he's nasty.
4   If he can't, he's weak.
5   He's not meant to be weak or nasty.
6   So he's not there.'

Activity 1

1   Create your own graffiti board with newspaper/ magazine cuttings that demonstrate the kinds of bad things that happen in the world. Separate these out into bad things caused by living beings and bad things caused by natural forces.

2   Try to write the problem of evil as expressed in Source 2 in even fewer words.

3   Search the Internet for stories that demonstrate people who have had lucky escapes or been in the wrong place at the wrong time. Is life just luck?

4   Discuss in your group times when you have thought 'It's not fair!' Explain what happened and why you thought it wasn't fair. What do other people think of your conclusion?

5   In religious belief, God is often said to be 'omnipotent', 'omniscient' and 'perfectly good'. Find out what each of these terms means and explain how each one is challenged by the problem of evil.

Source 3

Bob Evil isn't a thing, it's just a way of looking at something. You can't call an earthquake evil, it just is; it's a force of nature. You might as well call an apple falling from a tree evil.

Rob But if the apple smacks you on the head, then the apple isn't evil, but an evil thing has happened.

Bob I suppose, but do you really expect a God to stick his hand out and catch such an apple every time it's going to bounce off your head?

Rob Why not?

Bob Anyway, God's not going to interfere in our lives every time we choose to do something bad – we'd be his puppets then.

Rob So what, who would ever know? He could just replace our bad thoughts with good ones, and we'd never know we could have bad thoughts.

Bob But then we'd just be robots.

Rob Fine with me, at least we'd be robots who didn't suffer. And what about food? Why does everything we eat have to be a dead something else, or robbed from some other living thing?

Bob What's your alternative?

Rob Well, if God can do everything, why didn't he make it so that we can eat light, or air? Why does our survival depend on the deaths of other things? That's pretty evil in itself.

Bob I don't know that I would call it evil exactly …

Activity 2

1 Carry on Bob and Rob's conversation. Where do you think it might go next?

2 Do you think Bob or Rob is right? In pairs, take on the roles of Bob or Rob and justify your views about evil.

3 'All living things depend on the suffering of others for their survival.' Is this true? Discuss in class and see what conclusions you come to.

Source 4

'Evil comes in human form. There have always been bad people and there always will be. You can't blame God for the existence of evil people. Doing bad things is their choice, and you can't let them off the hook by claiming that it's all God's fault.'

'Well, actually, "bad people" aren't bad at all; they do bad things, but that's different. Everyone is a product of nature and nurture, a complicated mixture of what they were born with and the experiences they've had throughout life. You can't blame anyone for bad actions; we're all to blame. When someone does something wrong we've all played a part in making that happen.'

Source 5

'Natural evil isn't really evil at all; you might as well call a cold virus evil. It isn't, it's just a living thing surviving. It's just following the laws of nature which aren't evil, they're just laws. Gravity isn't evil, but you'll hurt yourself when you fall. It doesn't make any sense to say that natural evil proves there isn't a God because the laws of nature are what they are; they have nothing to do with whether there's a God or not. That's a completely different thing.'

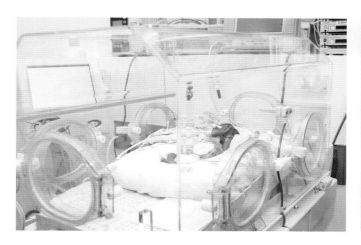

Activity 3

1   Discuss the kinds of evil actions humans do. When is something evil or not? How far do you think people's bad actions are under their control? Is it true that when people do bad things they shouldn't be blamed for them because it's all just because of how they were brought up or the DNA they got from their parents?

2   Imagine that a pill could be developed that would cancel out evil thoughts from your brain and so bring an end to evil caused by humans. Should criminals be forced to take this pill? Should everyone?

3   'Should God be blamed for evil?' Create a graffiti wall in your class where people can respond to this question.

11 Is belief in God compatible with the existence of evil?

Source 1

Yes it is: religious views

1 'One way to explain the existence of evil is just to say that God is not all the things we think he is: he's not all-powerful, he's just doing his best. We're trying to make God something he isn't and so we can't complain when he doesn't match up to the standard we have set for him.'

2 'No, I don't think we can do that. God is all-powerful and all-knowing, otherwise what kind of God would he be? I think evil exists for a purpose. Maybe it's to test us, or maybe there's some other reason. I wouldn't want to try to guess what God lets evil exist for. That's his business, not mine.'

3 'You just have to accept that free will is why evil happens. God made us like him: free and able to make our own decisions and face the consequences of our own actions. God isn't some big daddy in the sky keeping us right, that's for us to do. The existence of evil is the price we have to pay for being free.'

4 'God made the laws of physics; every now and then they cause problems. That's just the system, just the way things are. God can't change the laws of physics because then they wouldn't be laws and nothing would make any sense.'

5 'It may be a bit old fashioned to say this, but Satan is to blame. He causes evil and causes people to be evil. He made his free choice and now we just have to suffer for it. God even lets Satan have his way. That's freedom.'

Source 2

No, it's not: an atheist rejects Source 1

'What a collection of poor arguments. Let's take them one by one:

1 If God isn't all-powerful and all-good, what is he? If he's 'just trying his best' why on Earth should anyone worship him? No, the word 'God' is meant to mean all-powerful, all-good and so on. If not, how's that any kind of God?

2 Evil exists to test what exactly? Sounds like a nasty game show to me. And saying we don't know 'the reason'. What a cop-out!

3 Freedom is not a price worth paying at all, especially when the evil person isn't paying anything!

4 If God is God, he could have made the laws of physics a bit nicer. So why didn't he?

5 Satan? Come on! Why does God let Satan get away with this? Why does he let Satan even exist? Poor excuse, I think.'

Activity 1

1 In groups, take one of the arguments in Source 1 and discuss it. Your group should then be in the two-minute hot-seat where you are challenged by the class to justify the point of view.

2 'Dear Humans …'. Write a letter to humans from God where he explains the problem of evil and how it links to his existence.

3 Many people accept that there is evil in the world but also believe there is a god. What arguments, apart from the ones in Source 1, do you think they might give to support their beliefs?

4 Is Satan 'only an excuse'? Ask people in your school for their views about Satan. Do all religious people agree that he exists and that he is the cause of all evil?

5 Write your own religious answers in response to the atheist's comments in Source 2.

Source 3

'As a Hindu, I think the problem of evil has a simple solution. Our experiences in this life, good and bad, are the results of our actions in a previous life. This is the law of karma and samsara. As we go through our many incarnations, we build up karma as a result of our thoughts and actions. This karma keeps us on the endless cycle of birth, death and rebirth. As you move on through various incarnations in life, in each you are expected to progress to the next one by building up good karma, until the point where you can escape this cycle of birth, death and rebirth and become one with Brahman, the absolute, which is moksa. This will be the final release from all pain and suffering. So Brahman is not to blame for evil, our own actions are.'

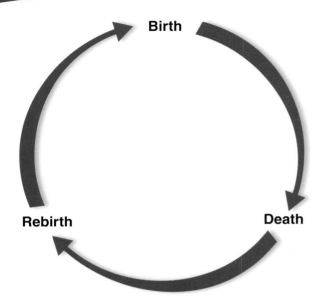

Birth

Death

Rebirth

Source 4

'We Buddhists believe that what happens to you in this life is also a result of the good and bad kamma you have built up in your previous forms. As you live you constantly create and recreate a pattern of yourself, which makes you what you are. You are formed from five skandhas, and it is these that you are constantly remaking, to become the "instructions" for the you that will exist next (maybe even in the next moment). As Buddhists, we do not believe that there is a God. Evil and suffering are just the results of causes and effects throughout life.'

The cycle of birth, death and rebirth

Activity 2

1 In what ways are Buddhism and Hinduism similar in the way they explain the existence of evil?

2 In pairs, compare the Buddhist and Hindu views in Sources 3 and 4 with the other arguments about the problem of evil you have studied in this chapter. Is it easier to explain away the problem of evil if you don't bring a God into it?

3 How do you think thoughts lead to actions? Is an evil thought as bad as an evil action? Are some evil thoughts and actions worse than others?

Source 5

'As a Christian, I think the only answer to the problem of evil is faith. Faith that God knows what he's doing and trust that he's doing what's right. How can we as humans explain the thoughts and actions of God? They are far beyond our understanding. I know evil exists, but I also know that God exists; one does not cancel out the other like some equation in maths. I have faith. That's all it comes down to really.'

'As a Humanist, I think the only answer to the problem of evil is that the existence of "evil" suggests that there is no divine figure up there controlling it all. If there was such a being, surely evil would not exist, but it does, and I can prove that. So on the one hand, I have something that can be seen and experienced; on the other hand there's a confused belief about the existence of some divine being who tolerates evil for some unknown purpose – far too many unknowns in my opinion.'

Activity 3

1 Go back through the material you have studied in this chapter. Design a set of revision cards that match up terms with definitions. For example, 'Infinite regress': 'The idea that if God created the universe something must have created God.'

2 Have a *Question Time* in your class where questions are asked about the existence of God. Each person on the 'panel' should be given a role, for example, a Humanist, a Christian, a Buddhist, etc.

3 Write your own reflective diary about how – if at all – your views have been challenged, changed or confirmed during your study of this chapter.

This section has given you the opportunity to explore a range of views on the question, 'Can we prove or disprove the existence of God?'

If you're doing the N5 exam, you'll be asked to show what you have learned about the **cosmological argument**, the **teleological argument** and the **problem of evil**, as well as religious and non-religious responses to these arguments.

You will also be expected to show that you can write about the strengths and weaknesses of the arguments, and the impact of the views you've studied on people's lives today.

Unlike a lot of assessments, the exam won't ask for specific viewpoints, so you will need to decide how to apply what you've learned.

Now try using what you've done in this section to answer the following exam-style questions.

Exam-style questions

1 'It's important for people to be able to work out if God is real or not.' **Joe**
   Give **two** reasons why Joe might say this.   **(4 KU)**

2 Explain what the cosmological argument says about the existence of God.   **(5 KU)**

3 Choose a religious viewpoint you have studied. Explain what it says about the need
   for a first cause.   **(5 KU)**

4 'A first cause is not necessary for the universe to exist.' What reasons might
   someone offer for this view?   **(6 KU)**

5 What observations might lead someone to believe that life and the universe
   were designed?   **(6 KU)**

6 Describe a non-religious response to the teleological argument.   **(6 KU)**

7 'If you accept what science says about how life got here, the design argument
   falls apart.' Is this true? Give reasons for your answer.   **(8 SKILLS)**

8 (a) What sorts of things might someone describe as 'evil'?   **(4 KU)**

   (b) Explain why these things might challenge a person's belief in the existence of God.   **(6 KU)**

   (c) 'When it comes to explaining the problem of evil, religious and non-religious people
        have nothing in common.' Is this true? Give reasons for your answer.   **(8 SKILLS)**

9 'The existence of evil proves God isn't real!' Do you agree? Give reasons for your answer.   **(8 SKILLS)**

10 Explain how deciding that there is no God might affect someone in their daily life.   **(4 SKILLS)**

11 'What you believe about the existence of God is down to how you interpret the evidence.
    We can never know for sure.' Do you agree? Give reasons for your answer.   **(8 SKILLS)**

Miracles

Source 1

It's a miracle!

'The death toll from the earthquake that took place in Ugistan just over 48 hours ago continues to rise as rescuers search among the rubble, listening for all they are worth for any signs of life beneath the wreckage of once towering buildings. Too often the silence is unbroken, and the removal of another piece of tortured masonry reveals another tragic soul whose life was taken far too early. However, occasionally signs of life are found and hope rises again. Just a few hours ago, a young girl's cries were heard from deep within a pile of brickwork, and rescuers carefully cleared the shattered debris to find her clinging to life, her life saved by the collapse of supporting metalwork in a way which protected her from being crushed. Locals in this deeply religious country are hailing these findings as miracles, a sure sign that the hand of God is at work. Prayers are being said for the safe delivery of many who as yet remain undiscovered and each welcome rescue is hailed as a little miracle in this sea of chaos.'

Source 2

'I have been unable to walk since childhood; an accident led to nerve damage. Doctors said I would never walk again and for almost 25 years that has been true. They did try various treatments, including new procedures and drugs of every shape and form, but none worked. It took time but I have learned to live with my condition; it just became part of who I am. A few years back, my mother died. She was a person of great faith and she always said to me that the good Lord would return my ability to walk when he felt that the time was right. I didn't share her beliefs and couldn't see why any God would be interested in putting something right he had allowed to happen in the first place. But when my mum died, I decided to honour her memory by trying out faith for myself. I became a Christian. A few months ago I attended a healing meeting with a pastor I'd never heard of. At the end of the service he called me up to the front and said very calmly, 'Perhaps the good Lord thinks it's time for you to walk again'. He touched my head and I fell down. Then I stood up and walked. Miracles do happen.'

A survivor being pulled from the rubble of a building in Port-au-Prince, Haiti, 2010

Miracles through faith

Activity 1

1 In pairs, think of as many questions as you can that you would like to ask about the stories in Sources 1 and 2.

2 Create a collage of newspaper headlines and images about the word 'miracle'. In this you should include some different views about what the word 'miracle' means.

3 Identify the evidence in Sources 1 and 2 that could be used by a religious person to support their belief that miracles exist.

4 Identify any possible evidence in Sources 1 and 2 that a non-religious person might use to question whether or not miracles exist.

5 'Miracles go against the laws of nature.' What does this phrase mean and what questions does it raise for you?

Source 3

'So what exactly do people mean by the word "miracle"? For some it is anything about life that fills them with wonder, for others it is something which they just can't explain because it seems "miraculous". For others it's something that goes against the known laws of physics. Because it doesn't have an explanation in nature, they think it has to be supernatural, i.e. the work of God, or the gods. Sacred scriptures include lots of accounts of miracles where divine beings act, either directly or through specially chosen people. Some argue that it isn't reasonable to expect miracles in the modern world, but for others miracles are not just a thing of the past. After all, if miracles did take place in the past, why shouldn't they *still* happen today?'

Activity 2

1 Spend some time online collecting modern examples of things people have seen as miraculous. Try to find examples from at least two different religions, but you can include examples that aren't connected to a particular religion too. They might be big dramatic events, or quieter, more personal things.

2 Rewrite the stories in your own words, and bring them together to create a 'Little Book of Modern Miracles'. Keep a copy to refer to as you work through this section.

3 As you share the stories you have found, discuss the following questions:

- Do the events you have found fit the definitions of a miracle given in Source 3?
- How might religious people explain them?
- How might non-religious people explain them?
- Do you think religious and non-religious people will always see these events differently?

Source 4

'Miracles are real. There's just no way to explain how some things have happened otherwise. They might be people being healed or having narrow escapes from death; how can you explain how "lucky" people seem to be in some situations in any other way? And why shouldn't they happen? Faith is about believing that anything is possible, and that it doesn't always have to have a reasonable explanation. It's about accepting that sometimes things can't be explained in the normal ways and that we have to look for explanations that are beyond natural – supernatural, I suppose. I mean, if it is possible to accept that a God created the entire universe and has power over it, then why would it be difficult to accept that such a being could heal an illness or save a person from danger? Besides, not believing in miracles is a belief in itself, isn't it? Why is it any more strange for the laws of nature to be bent every now and again than for them to be a law unto themselves all the time?'

Modern-day miracles

Source 5

'I think we need to get right what we mean by a miracle. There are some things that might seem like miracles, but are just examples of the different ways we see things. For example, imagine someone from a thousand years ago was transported to the twenty-first century. What would she think about the world as it is now? What would tablets and the Internet look like to her? What would the ability to talk to someone on a mobile phone look like to her? For that matter, what would switching on a light bulb look like to her? All of these things would look like miracles: humans having power over nature; humans controlling their world in ways that would not have been possible in her day. Miracles are just delusion, misunderstanding or simply that we can't explain things yet – nothing more.'

Activity 3

1   What do you understand by the word 'supernatural'? What problems are there with believing that things can be 'supernatural'?

2   Make a list of things that people might describe as miracles. Now think of as many different explanations for each one as you can.

3   'You cannot be a religious person unless you believe in miracles.' Use sticky notes on a whiteboard to express your own views on this statement.

Source 6

'The trouble with a miracle is that for every miracle there are many more "not miracles". For every person "miraculously" saved from danger and death in some terrible situation, there are many more who were not saved from danger or death. If we say that the people saved are examples of miracles and so support religious beliefs, does that mean that the people who were not saved count against religious belief? You can't have it both ways; if you think miracles are evidence for the existence of a God, then all the bad things that are not saved by a miracle must be evidence against the existence of a God. Or maybe he just likes to save some people with a miracle and not others; what kind of a God would that be? No, miracles are just an example of wishful thinking.'

Activity 4

1   How do you think a religious person would respond to the view in Source 4 (on page 41)?

2   Create a piece of artwork in which you express your views about what miracles are and whether or not they exist.

3   Use the letters in the word 'miracle' to make an acrostic explaining a religious person's and a non-religious person's views about miracles. For example, for a religious person: M is for 'miracle', a thing that God does; I is for 'incredible', which miracles are … And for a non-religious person: M is for 'miracle', a thing which is all in the mind; I is for 'interpretation', which means that you interpret something perfectly ordinary as something extraordinary …

Source 1

Miracles in the Old Testament

There are many different miracles in the Old Testament. Some are miracles concerning nature, some concerning people, some to help win battles or even conceive children when that seemed impossible. Some are part of a bigger story where God shows his power.

- Lot's wife turned into a pillar of salt (Genesis 19:26)
- The burning bush (Exodus 3:2)
- The plagues (Numbers 16:46–50)
- Balaam's donkey speaks (Numbers 22:23–30)
- The sun and moon stand still (Joshua 10:12–14)
- Jonah inside the whale (Jonah 1:17; 2:10)

The story of Lot's wife from Genesis 19:26

Source 2

Miracles in the New Testament

In the same way, the miracles in the New Testament are very varied. Most are carried out by Jesus and some of these involve healing or even raising the dead. Others involve power over natural forces. Some are carried out by the Holy Spirit and involve giving people powers. Of course, perhaps the most important miracle of all in the New Testament is when Jesus returns from the dead.

- Jesus turns water into wine: John 2:1–11
- Jesus heals a blind man: Mark 8:22–26
- Jesus feeds five thousand: Matthew 14:13–21
- Jesus raises Lazarus: John 11:1–45
- Jesus walks on water: Mark 6:45–52

Jesus heals a blind man from Mark 8:22–26

Activity 1

1 Choose one of the miracle stories from Sources 1 and 2 (on page 43) and re-present this story in the form of a news item for TV news. You should include comment in your item about the range of views that people are likely to have about this story.

2 Miracle Scene Investigation 1. You have been asked to investigate one of the miracle stories in Sources 1 and 2. How would you go about this? What questions would you ask and who would you ask? What kinds of research into the story do you think you would use?

3 Choose a different miracle from those listed in Sources 1 and 2. Make a list of 'alternative explanations' for this event. Ask people in your class for their ideas about alternative explanations for the events in the story.

4 You have been asked to tell one of the miracle stories to a group of Primary 2 children. How would you go about doing this in a way that allowed them to ask questions about the story?

5 Have a look at the class's list of 'alternative explanations' in task 3 above. How might a range of different religious people respond to each of these 'alternative explanations'?

Source 3

'As a Christian, I think we have to accept the miracles in the Bible for what they are: evidence of God's power and that Jesus was, in fact, his son. We really can't start saying "that miracle happened and that one didn't" just because they seem to go against our scientific way of thinking in the twenty-first century. If we start doing that, then we might as well just forget about the Bible completely and make up our own faith as we go along. Miracles are part of the mystery of our faith. We can't analyse them like you would analyse chemicals, it's not like that. We have to accept that they happened as the Bible says they did.'

Source 4

'As a Christian, I think we have to be careful about how we understand the miracles in the Bible. Remember that the Bible was written by people, and those people had a story to tell and claims to make. They were trying to show that God has power and that Jesus was God in human form. Perhaps they exaggerated a little from time to time for effect. Perhaps, too, the stories were handed down through the generations and got more and more miraculous as time went on. Bible times were different to how things are now; people had a different view of the world and a different way of understanding it. So we should treat the miracle stories for what they are: stories that are part of the message of our faith, not to be taken literally or too seriously. And no, I don't think that makes my faith weak; if anything it makes it stronger, because I can believe without having to accept every word in the Bible as true.'

Activity 2

1 In your own words, summarise the similarities and differences between the two Christian views in Sources 3 and 4.

2 Write and perform a dialogue that these two Christians might have.

3 In your dialogue, you could add views from someone who is not religious. How would they respond to both of these beliefs? Would they challenge one more than the other and how would they do so?

'When I was younger I remember learning about the story of the raising of Lazarus from the dead. I remember thinking at the time that you could look at the story in many different ways. On the one hand it was the ultimate demonstration of the power of Jesus and must have brought great comfort to Lazarus' family, but on the other hand, you could think of it as quite a cruel way for Jesus to show his power. How did Lazarus feel being taken from heaven and brought back to life? Was it right to do this without his permission, just to show Jesus' power? And anyway, Lazarus must have died at some point so it was only putting off the inevitable; in fact, it meant that Lazarus had to die twice. In what way is that an act of kindness? The story leaves me with big questions about the whole idea of miracles.'

Activity 3

1   How would a Christian respond to the viewpoint in Source 5?

2   Should Christians stop believing in miracles and just concentrate on the teachings of their religion and following its guidance for living a good life? Discuss in class and create a graffiti wall about your class views.

3   Create a Wordle™ image using text you have written about Christian beliefs about miracles. Which words appear most often and what does this tell you about Christian beliefs about miracles?

Source 1

The life of the Buddha is full of miracles. In fact, the birth of Siddartha Gautama, who would become the Buddha, comes itself with a heavy dose of miraculous happenings. It is said that his mother dreamed that a white elephant entered her side and this was followed by the birth of a child who seemed to have an unnatural level of understanding right from birth. Throughout the life of the Buddha, other miracles followed: according to some, he was able to read people's minds, use his 'third eye' to see beyond normal sight, multiply his body many times and fly through space. For many Buddhists, these miracles point to a being who was far more than human.

Buddha's 'third eye' can be seen in the middle of his forehead

Source 2

'There are some branches of the Buddhist faith where modern miracles are very much part of belief. Some Buddhists don't really get into these beliefs, and some don't think they happen at all, but there are beliefs about supernatural happenings in Buddhism which, although they might not be miracles in the same way as those in Christianity, definitely involve changes to the laws of physics which I suppose makes them miraculous. For example, some believe that at certain stages of enlightenment, some high Buddhist lamas may travel outside of their body in a spiritual realm, or even carry out activities with only the power of their minds like some kind of extra-sensory perception. However, some Buddhists really don't go with these ideas at all.'

Activity 1

1 Illustrate one of the miracles of Buddhism.
2 Miracle Scene Investigation 2. Carry out a similar investigation into one of the miracles of Buddhism just as you did for biblical miracles in Chapter 14. What questions would you ask? What evidence would you look for?
3 Come up with a list of alternative explanations for one of the miracles of Buddhism.
4 You have to explain one of the miracles of Buddhism to a group of adults who are interested in Buddhism. How would you 'explain' the place of miracles in Buddhism?
5 Script a dialogue between two Buddhists: one who believes that miracles are an important part of Buddhist belief and one who does not.

Source 3

'For me, belief in miracles is not something you need to have as a Buddhist. Buddhism is more of a philosophy for me rather than a set of supernatural beliefs. Yes, of course the Buddha may well have been able to carry out actions that we would think of as miraculous – who can say – but that's not what's important in his message. What matters is what he taught, the example he set in his life and how he pointed the way for all of us to escape the endless cycles of birth and rebirth. Besides, what would be the point of a miracle for a Buddhist? A healing miracle; pain and suffering are just as much illusions as comfort and happiness.'

Source 4

'For me, belief in miracles is an important part of my belief in the role of the Buddha in my belief-system. After all, the Buddha is said to have had many previous incarnations, sometimes as a human and sometimes as an animal. Now if Buddha can live life as an animal and go through many forms of existence, that in itself is miraculous. Also, in my kind of Buddhism we believe in the existence of Boddhisattvas and demi-gods who can influence human lives if we ask them to. This means that they can break into the laws of physics of the natural world and change them if need be; that's surely miraculous. Yes, some Buddhists think of Buddhism as just a kind of philosophy, but I don't. It's a religion, and belief in the supernatural is an important part of any religion, Buddhism included.'

A Bodhisattva

Activity 2

1 In your own words, summarise the similarities and differences between the two Buddhist views in Sources 3 and 4.

2 Write and perform the kind of conversation these two Buddhists might have.

3 Which of these two Buddhist viewpoints would a non-religious person be more likely to challenge? How would they do this?

Source 5

'I'm an atheist, and so are Buddhists, but they have a religion and I don't. I know, it's a bit confusing. My response to miracles in Buddhism is exactly the same as my response to miracles in any religion. Why are they necessary? Why do they seem to happen sometimes and not others? Is there some kind of table drawn up where a miracle would be OK here but not there? Why would one person surviving some terrible disaster be counted as a miracle when the fact that all the others who didn't "miraculously" survive don't count against belief in miracles? Miracles are just the leftovers of old superstitions and have no place in the modern world whether you're religious or not.'

Activity 3

1 From what you have studied about Buddhism, would you agree that a Buddhist is an atheist?

2 What are the differences and similarities between Christian and Buddhist views about miracles? Do you think it is possible to follow one of these religions and not believe in miracles?

3 Create a Wordle™ image for Buddhist beliefs about miracles in the same way that you did for Christianity in Chapter 14. In what ways are the two similar or different?

Source 1

'Just think about how little we really know about the universe and how it works. Just think about how vast the universe is and how we're discovering new things about it all the time. I mean, we don't even fully understand the workings of the human brain yet! Just think about how often we have thought about something one way at one time and then gone on to think about it differently at another time. So why exactly is believing in miracles such a big deal? For religious people their scriptures are true, not in some wishy-washy way, but in an actual, literal way. How would you even start to pick and choose which bits you can believe in and which bits you're not going to believe in? Religion isn't a supermarket where you choose one brand over another, nor is it a lump of clay which you can mould however you like. It is what it is, and if it includes stories of miracles, then you simply have to believe them. That's the deal.'

Source 2

'I believe in a God whose power has no limits. I believe in a God who knows things in a way that I could never know them. I believe in a God who knows what is, what has been and what will be. I believe in a God who knows what's best always, not just sometimes. I believe in a God who makes his own decisions for his own reasons, and who doesn't have to ask for my permission or my understanding first. I believe in a God who does things that may look like one thing to me, but that might actually be something different. I believe in a God who is God after all and I am not. All of which means that I believe in miracles: totally, absolutely and without question. That's what faith means.'

The first Pentecost

Activity 1

1 Using Sources 1 and 2, write three things you agree with in these sources and three things you disagree with. Now compare the agreements and disagreements across your class.

2 Many Christians believe that everything in the Bible is literally true. Have a look at the following stories in the Bible and think about how believing in them as literally true might cause problems for believers. How do you think they deal with these possible problems?

- The story of Noah
- The wives of Adam and Eve's children
- The tower of Babel
- Jesus walking on water
- The events at the first Pentecost.

3 What are the benefits and problems, in your opinion, with the belief that 'God knows best'? Discuss in class and create a display of your thinking.

4 Some people argue that you should not 'pick and mix' your religion, but that you have to choose one and follow it all. What do you think about this view?

5 Some religious people think that believing in the literal truth of the Bible shows stronger faith than not taking everything literally. Others think the opposite. What do you think?

Source 3

'Sometimes people think that if you believe that miracles are literally true you have somehow put your brain on the shelf and become some unthinking thing with its head in the sand. Well, I don't think that's true at all. Take love, hope, loyalty and friendship; they're not things, they are ways of looking at things based on what we see. We see their effects and so we explain these effects by giving them names. Could anyone say "I don't believe in love" because it's not something you can see directly? (You can't see intelligence either for that matter, just what it does.) Miracles are no different from that. You see their effect and you say they are either miracles from God or coincidence or mind over matter; every one of these choices is just that – a choice.'

Source 4

'Actually, science doesn't disprove that miracles are possible at all. In fact, maybe the opposite is true. How? Well, here goes. Nowadays, we can do things that would seem like miracles to people long ago. If you believe, like I do, that Jesus was God in human form, then he knows everything including things people didn't know then but know now. So, that means that he didn't have to change the laws of physics to do a miracle, just apply skills that we only have now (or still don't have) at a time when those skills were unknown to others; that would then be defined as a miracle. Take bringing people back from the dead, for example. Nowadays, scientists can achieve this by using CPR and chemical injections among other things. Is it possible that Jesus just used such skills that others would have no knowledge of and this looked like a miracle? If that is so, then his miracles were miraculous, just not changes to the laws of physics. So, I believe they were literally true, but that can still mean that they were something different from what people say they were.'

Activity 2

1 In addition to intelligence, love, hope, loyalty and friendship, what other things do you think are 'invisible and yet real'?

2 Do you think the people in Sources 3 and 4 really believe in miracles? Discuss in class.

3 Create a series of cards that include arguments for and against belief in miracles. Each card should have only one argument for or against. Now shuffle the cards and see who can match up each for and against quickest.

'People believe in the power of wishing wells, in good and bad luck, in UFOs and little green men from outer space. Some athletes believe that unless they perform a certain set of rituals before they compete they will lose. People believe that you should touch wood after you say something so you're not tempting fate. People believe that the number 13 is unlucky. Now how reasonable are all of these things? Not very, I'd say. So why is it that people jump at the chance to write off miracles because they are linked to religion? Simple answer: it's because they're against religion in the first place and they think miracles give them another excuse to slag off religion. I believe that my religion is true, and I believe that miracles happen. I don't need evidence or argument.'

Activity 3

1 Carry out your own survey into the extent to which people still believe in things that might be called 'superstitions'. Which are most commonly believed? How much do people really believe in them? You can display your findings.

2 Why do you think people believe in the supernatural? Create your own word wall which offers suggestions.

3 Some religious people would say that unless you believe in the literal truth of miracles you cannot call yourself a true believer. What do you think?

Are you superstitious about any of these things?

Source 1

'For me, miracles are something that modern Christians shouldn't really bother too much about. The ones in the Bible should be seen for what they were: stories written to show the power of God and Jesus. People were far more superstitious then and so it made sense to tell stories that they would take notice of. I don't have to believe that Jesus walked on water – I mean, why would he? – to believe in his message. My Christianity is a very practical thing, and it's based on the teachings and life of Jesus, not that he did things that look more like magic tricks than the teachings of a man who understood the world and human nature. As for modern miracles, there's always going to be a rational explanation for those and Christians will just have to keep explaining them away as science explains them better and better. I don't need miracles to believe.'

Source 2

'I believe in miracles and at the same time I don't believe in miracles. I know that sounds like I'm contradicting myself, but I'm not. You see, I believe that what we call a miracle did happen, but that it's not an example of breaking the laws of physics which I don't think God would do. Why make laws then break them when you feel like it? That's hardly a good example from the Almighty. No, miracles happened, but we need to be clear about what they were. Take the feeding of the five thousand. Did Jesus miraculously multiply loaves and fish to feed five thousand people? No, the people brought their own lunch (as you'd expect them to, after all). Then, after listening to Jesus, they realised that they should share what little they had – with complete strangers. That shared thinking – that we are all responsible for each other – is the true miracle. So the "miracle" did happen, but not the way we think it did.'

Activity 1

1 Write the statement 'For me, miracles are something that modern Christians shouldn't really bother about' on a whiteboard. Now add points of view about this statement, including views you think different Christians might have about this.

2 Choose some of the miracles you have looked at in this chapter. For each one, describe what you think might be a 'rational' explanation for that miracle. Are there some miracles that seem more rational than others?

3 Take your list of miracles from task 2 and write each miracle and its 'rational explanation' on a card. Now try to match them up. Do some miracles have the 'same rational explanation'?

4 Discuss the view in Source 2 (on page 51). Do you think this person is just trying to 'explain away' miracles?

5 Does not believing in the literal truth of miracles mean you have a strong faith or a weak one?

Source 3

'Someone today rises up and walks despite doctors telling them they would never walk again. Someone is cured from some disease and doctors can't explain how it happened. Yes, these are miracles, but changes to the laws of physics? No. The miracle is that somehow a person's beliefs are so strong that in some unknown way they cure themselves. That is the miracle of the power of belief, not some reorganisation of the laws of nature. So I can still believe in miracles, but I can believe in them in a way which means that the laws of physics don't get altered by God according to some whim of his.'

Source 4

'The trouble with miracles is that they come in so many shapes and forms and so it makes more sense to explain each one in turn individually. I don't have a problem with Jesus rising from the dead; that was a one-off, part of the whole story. I can even believe that people today experience "miraculous" healings, though what these actually are, I'm not sure. But weeping statues; the face of Jesus miraculously appearing on a piece of toast; a vision of a religious figure floating in the air, with a new message for mankind? For me, all of that is out-of-date superstition, expectation and interpretation, and Christianity can do without it.'

Source 5

'Believing in miracles in the twenty-first century? You might as well believe in the tooth fairy, Santa, and goblins at the bottom of the garden. Believing in miracles is something that modern religious people should abandon, and quickly. Nothing else in your religious faith has to be thrown away if you stop believing in miracles. They are mind over matter, strange coincidences, ways of looking at things that can be viewed one way or another. They are evidence of nothing more than how gullible people can be – yes, including religious people. For me, they are a bit of an embarrassment, something I keep having to explain away. And then people say "Ah, but how can you be a Christian then if you don't believe in miracles?" But I can. I believe that Jesus was God's son, and that if everyone followed his moral teaching the world would be a better place. I don't need to believe in the hocus-pocus stuff as well.'

Activity 2

1 If miracles are just 'the power of belief', might a miracle not happening make someone believe their belief is not good enough? Discuss this and note down any views you have.

2 All Christians believe that Jesus literally died and rose from the dead; that is a miracle. So do you think Christians who understand miracles as metaphors are contradicting themselves when they say the resurrection was a literal miracle, but all the other miracles are metaphorical ones?

3 What do you think is meant by the statement in Source 4 that belief in miracles is about 'superstition, expectation and interpretation'?

Activity 3

1 How you understand miracles is about the differences between reason and faith. What do you think the differences are between these concepts? Can you base your beliefs on reason and faith, or does it have to be one or the other? Think, pair, share on this one!

2 Should religious people bring up their children to believe in Santa and the tooth fairy? How might this cause problems for a child's belief in miracles (or when they 'grow out' of believing in Santa, for example)?

3 From a religion you have studied, how much of it depends on belief in supernatural things? Should all religions do away with the supernatural parts of their faith? Would that make them more reasonable? Would that require more or less faith?

Miracles: a psychological approach

Source 1

'Mind over matter, no matter whether it is a miracle in the Bible or a modern-day one. All you are seeing is the power of the human brain to create situations which are then understood as miracles. Hypnosis has been used to make people see and believe all sorts of things. It has even been used to cancel out feelings of pain during medical treatment. Now, if the brain can do this, then surely it can do other things which might then look to someone as if they are divine actions. For example, many of the healing miracles in the Bible might have been psychosomatic illnesses; all that was needed to cure them was a little cognitive reorganisation, getting the brain to "unthink" these illnesses. I think almost all modern miracles are an example of this; the power of prayer is much more the power of suggestion and of tricking your brain into a new set of beliefs.'

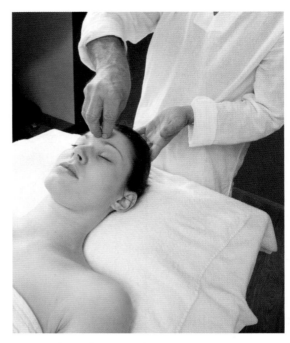

A person being hypnotised

Source 2

'I don't think you even have to go that far. Miracles are just a case of seeing something the way you want to see it, a kind of mass hysteria. It's a bit like this: imagine you're sitting alone in your house on a dark night. You hear a noise outside. Now, let's say you've just watched a scary movie. You'll be far more likely to think that the noise outside was a serial killer than a pigeon flying into your window. In the same way, people who witness or experience miracles expect them to happen — they will them to happen — and they take their cues from the reactions of others. This expectation means that they will give anything the name "miracle" if it matches up with what they expected to happen and others seem to agree.'

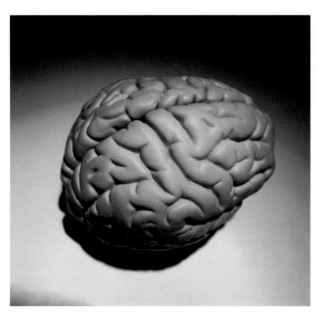

A human brain

Activity 1

1 Find out about the medical uses of hypnosis. Could this be an explanation for any of the biblical miracles or any modern miracles?

2 Some people think that prayer is just a form of self-hypnosis. What do you think?

3 The 'Toronto Blessing' was first hailed as a miraculous blessing of the gifts of the Holy Spirit, then quite quickly rejected by many Christians as something else entirely. Find out about this event and discuss how it might be an example of mass hysteria as opposed to any kind of miracle.

4 Go back and look at the healing miracles of Jesus in Chapter 14. Which of these could be explained as psychosomatic illness? Which might be explained as Jesus treating a psychosomatic illness?

5 Psychologists could argue that a miracle is both an example of social learning theory as well as the power of reinforcement. Find out what these terms mean and think about how they might apply to one or more of the miracles you have studied so far.

Source 3

'The human brain is designed to see patterns and make sense of them. It is designed to look for meaning behind things, even when there is no meaning. It likes to give order and structure to things that are just random. Imagine someone said to you, "I want you to remember that time when you lost a balloon you were carrying in the street". Now maybe you've never lost a balloon, but your brain will struggle hard to make this story fit with something you have experienced; maybe you'll remember losing a balloon when you didn't or you'll think of something kind of like a balloon you lost when you were a child. It's like seeing faces in the clouds; it's just random patterns but your brain tries to make sense of them by 'seeing' a face. That's all miracles are: your brain making something out of nothing.'

Source 4

'Wishful thinking and wish fulfilment, that's what miracles are. We want something to happen so much that we believe it has happened. This is a kind of self-trickery to help us match up what we wanted to happen with what actually happened. This helps us make sense of our world, justifies our beliefs and positively reinforces them. We then report these to others and before you know it, our perception about what happened becomes an established fact. Pple wnat thri bilefs to be tuer so strlgly thit I thnk the jst fit whaot thy se inato what theiy waounted to siaee and confuse the two so completely that they even fool themselves. Jesus' followers desperately wanted him to be the Messiah, they desperately wanted him to be able to do miracles; so what they wanted to see, they saw. The same applies today: people want so badly to believe that God can heal that they give any healing that is not 100 per cent explained by science the label "miracle". And so the myths go on.'

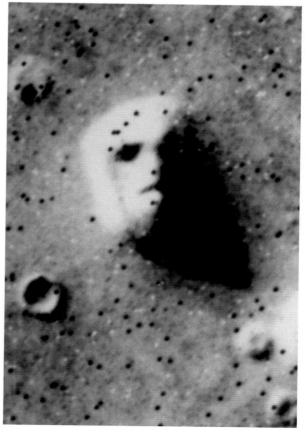

The 'face on Mars'

Activity 2

1 Search on the Internet for the 'face on Mars'. How might this example of the brain trying to make sense of what it sees be linked to the idea of miracles? What about making sense of some of the text in Source 4 (on page 55)?

2 Which of the miracles you have looked at might be seen as 'wish fulfilment'? Why do people want to believe, and how can this affect their actual experiences?

3 What other examples of 'self-trickery' might your brain engage in? (And why?)

Source 5

'Have you ever walked right past someone you know well, then said "I didn't see you" when you actually meant that you did see them but didn't register that you saw them? Psychologists report the concept of "inattention blindness", where we literally don't recognise what's before our eyes (Simons & Chabris, 1999). People can watch videos where a gorilla walks right in front of the camera, but they have no memory of seeing it. In fact they did see it, they just didn't consciously register it. This suggests that the brain is fantastically complex, and so sometimes we don't see what's right in front of us. So when we "see" or "experience" something miraculous, what are we actually seeing (or missing) and experiencing (or thinking we are experiencing)? Could it be that a miracle is just us registering what we choose to register, or not registering what is actually there?'

Activity 3

1 Look up 'inattention blindness' on YouTube and discuss the videos that appear. (The psychologist Richard Wiseman has a lot to say about this.) Could inattention blindness explain our belief in miracles?

2 Some have suggested that 'miracles' are a complicated mixture of expectation, wish fulfilment and simple illusion. Which of the miracle stories you have looked at so far could fit into one or more of these categories?

Source 1

'Oh here we go again, attacks on religion from the "science" of psychology. I mean, these are people who think that you can measure personality, intelligence and all sorts of things that are just plain daft. Some of them still even follow the teachings of Sigmund Freud; what more do I need to say? You can't really do an experiment to prove or disprove a miracle. There's no questionnaire or interview that will really get to the bottom of it. So perhaps psychologists should just stick to what they're best at, and leave religion out of it. They just seem to think that people are more like particularly gullible sheep, and that we're all so easily fooled. The first disciples took on the might of the Roman Empire; would they have done that because they had experienced an illusion of the risen Christ? I don't think so. Yes, people can be deceived, but not about what really matters.'

Source 2

'There's no doubt that psychology can give us very helpful insights into the tricky world of human experience. There's no doubt that it can suggest alternative explanations for people who have seen or experienced a miracle. There's no doubt that it can show us examples of where people have got it very wrong and claimed to have seen or experienced something that wasn't there. But it can only suggest these alternative explanations, it can't prove them to be true. Perhaps the people who witnessed biblical miracles really were deluded, maybe they really were the victims of very clever illusions, maybe the power of suggestion and expectation really did overcome them. But we'll never know, because we can't go back and give them psychological tests.'

Sigmund Freud

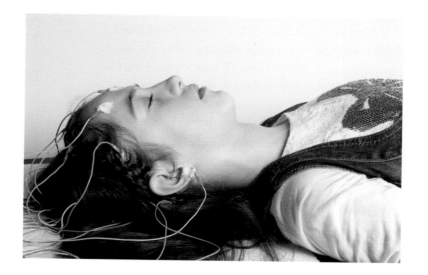

Activity 1

1 Find out how psychologists try to measure personality and intelligence. Can these things be measured? Are psychologists going about it in the right way? Can psychologists measure everything?

2 Carry out some research into the theories of Sigmund Freud. What did he say about religion? Create a display of your findings.

3 'The first disciples didn't need to see Jesus come back from the dead, they just had to believe that's what they saw.' Write this on a whiteboard and get people in your class to add their comments.

4 Do the miracles of Jesus *have to be* true?

5 Some religious people argue that miracles can only be perceived by a 'sixth sense' – one that is spiritual and not physical. What do you think of this?

Source 3

'No matter what psychology says, miracles remain a belief. And if that belief helps you in your life, what good does it do to pick it apart and chip away at it all the time? If you are comforted by your belief in miracles, if that belief helps you to make sense of a scary world, then why should anyone waste time trying to knock your belief in miracles? What harm does it do for anyone to believe in a miracle? Is believing in miracles a threat to world peace and global stability? I don't think so. In that case, let people believe in miracles; what does it matter to anyone else? Why do so many "new atheists" use sciences like psychology to back up their beliefs when it suits them?'

Source 4

'There's probably no explanation, so stop worrying and enjoy your life'

'Psychologists, like all scientists, come up with one explanation one day and the opposite a week later. One theory says this and one theory says that. Imagine a world where psychology was our religion; we'd be turning round and round, week after week, not knowing what to think or which piece of research to believe. At least religion is quite clear in its explanations, and quite consistent. It troubles me when modern religious people try to bend their faith to fit in with the latest trends, fashions and bits of science. Your faith should be like an anchor – something that holds you – not something you change all the time to fit in with whatever's cool. Psychologists have got no more of a clue about what a miracle is or isn't and whether they are real or not than anyone else, so stop worrying, believe in miracles and enjoy your life.'

Activity 2

1 A psychologist has been accused of causing harm to people's cherished beliefs. What defence might the psychologist offer?

2 Does the fact that psychology – like all sciences – has many conflicting theories make it easier or harder for it to challenge belief in miracles?

3 Should science spend any time challenging belief in miracles?

'Let's say that a time machine was invented and its occupant went back and followed the life of Jesus from beginning to end. The time traveller returns to the present day to tell us that all the miracle stories of Jesus never happened at all, or have perfectly reasonable explanations in terms of human behaviour. So, would Christianity crumble to nothing? I don't think so. You see, religious belief is much bigger than that. In fact, maybe one of the tests of the strength of religious belief is that it no longer lives in a "childish" world where, if "magical" things don't happen, the religion means nothing. If science gave us utterly believable explanations for every miracle claim there has ever been, that would have no effect on my belief. You see, my belief doesn't depend on proof or falsehood, it depends on belief. So, no scientific explanation can count for or against my belief.'

Activity 3

1 Would this time traveller's evidence be enough to bring Christianity to an end? Discuss and note any interesting views raised.

2 'Science deals with facts and religion deals with beliefs. You can't mix the two, it would be like mixing oil and water.' What do you think?

3 How far do you think psychology challenges the existence of miracles?

Source 1

Hume's argument goes like this:

A miracle is something that 'violates the laws of nature'. Given that the laws of nature are fixed – not to mention incredibly powerful – if we are going to accept something as a violation of a law of nature then the evidence for it has to be pretty extraordinary. Like all claims, we have to balance up the evidence in favour of it and the evidence against it. Claims that laws of nature have been violated are very strong claims, so obviously the supporting evidence needs to be very strong as well. There is an awful lot of evidence to suggest that laws of nature are fixed, and not subject to change. So, when it is claimed that a law of nature has been violated – as in the case of a miracle – it makes far more sense to believe that the miracle didn't happen at all and that, in fact, the person who is claiming that a miracle happened is just making a mistake.

What is this a picture of?

Source 2

Hume's argument is based on the idea of empirical evidence, that is, evidence from experience. When we judge empirical evidence, we have to ask ourselves what counts and what does not. Let's say that we include what we see as reliable empirical evidence, but is it? This would mean that 'seeing is believing', but is that true? What about feelings and experiences as empirical evidence, are they reliable? Maybe the only reliable empirical evidence is solid evidence like a photograph, which can't lie or get it wrong. Or can it? We still need to interpret what we 'see' in a photograph! We do have to remember that Hume was writing a long time ago, before the rise of much of what we call 'modern science'; his argument is philosophical, not scientific, so we have to take it that way.

Activity 1

1   Look back at the miracles you have studied in this section. Which ones are most likely to be called 'violations of the laws of nature'?

2   Some people reject miracles because the laws of nature cannot be broken, even by God. What do you think? Could God break a law of nature and, if so, what use are the laws of nature?

3   What things do you accept based only on empirical evidence? Are there things you are prepared to accept without empirical evidence? Is empirical evidence the best form of evidence?

4   Can a photograph lie?

5   If a miracle is a violation of a law of nature, does this mean that it has to come from God (or a god)?

Source 3

Hume was particularly challenging about the role of individual testimony in miracle stories. He questioned how far we should accept one person's (or more than one person's) account of a miracle, when all the everyday empirical evidence points to the individual's experience being wrong (or misguided). Perhaps religious people want to tell miracle stories for perfectly good reasons, but that's not to say they are true. On the other hand, to accept that a miracle is true based on one person's experience is pretty shaky ground. Would we then have to accept everyone's testimony about everything? Should we give some sort of priority to miracle stories because they are religious stories?

David Hume

Source 4

Hume also pointed out that we need to remember how difficult it is to establish the facts of things that happened long ago; it's not easy to disentangle what actually happened from what was reported to have happened. He also suggests that civilisations in the past were very different from nowadays; superstition and 'miraculous' events were much more likely to be accepted by people in the past than they are now. Hume points out that societies develop from more to less superstitious as time goes on, and that as we get a better understanding of the way the world works, we become less likely to explain things as miracles. Hume was actually pretty harsh about those in the past who claimed to have witnessed or experienced a miracle, saying that 'in all history there never has been a sufficient number of people of unquestioned good sense, education, learning, reputation and undoubted integrity to persuade us that they were not deluding themselves or deceiving others'.

Activity 2

1   What might make a person's individual report of a miracle reliable or unreliable? How much trust should we put in someone's claim that a miracle has happened?

2   Because we can't prove what actually happened in biblical times (or in the past generally) should we give up trying?

3   What other examples do you know of where a society moves from more to less superstitious through time?

Source 5

Finally, Hume said that people are too ready to believe in miracles. This is because there's something in human nature that makes us like to believe that there is more to life than meets the eye. So, for example, think about the last time you exaggerated something. Why did you do it? It's likely that you puffed your story up a bit because the real story was a bit ordinary and boring: adding a little colour and imagination made your story more likely to be listened to and more interesting for listeners. Hume thought that miracle stories were just 'embellishments' that never happened. Maybe they're just exaggerations to make us feel better about ourselves, or to make our world seem more interesting, or the people about whom the miracle stories are concerned more interesting.

Activity 3

1 Why might people be too ready to believe in miracles?

2 When did you last exaggerate? Is exaggeration a lie?

3 Design your own factsheet on Hume's views of miracles and leave space on this for religious responses, which you'll cover in the next section.

Source 1

'The easiest way to respond to Hume's argument is by using swans. Let me explain. Let's say that I make the claim "all swans are white". How could I possibly prove this? Well, the simplest answer is to go and count them all. But of course, by the time I'd gone round the world counting, many new swans would have hatched, any one of which might be black (or tartan, for all I know). So, let's say everyone on the planet agrees that at twelve minutes past six on the same day we'll all track down every swan in the world simultaneously. Who could prove that we hadn't missed the green swan hiding in the bushes? No, it's not possible to disprove (or falsify) the statement "all swans are white", so equally, it's not possible to prove (or disprove) the statement "miracles don't exist". Cheerio Hume!'

Source 2

'I believe that God is omnipotent. That means all-powerful; he's a he-can-do-anything sort of being. So, being omnipotent, that means he can do what he wants when he wants, and that includes miracles. And yes, he can even do something that would be logically impossible, like create something that he couldn't uncreate (but that would be silly and God is all-knowing). So, for humans it might seem logically impossible for God to carry out a miracle but the point is that God can do something logically impossible if he wants to; that's omnipotence for you after all. Now why God would do so sometimes and not others, that's a different question. But the point is that God can "violate the laws of nature" if he wants; they're his laws. God one, Hume nil.'

Activity 1

1 Create your own display on the 'all swans are white' argument. Display this at a parents' evening and engage those who come to view your display in discussion about it. Perhaps you could start by asking them if there could be such a thing as a tartan swan.

2 If you can't prove or disprove miracles, should we stop talking about them altogether? Think, pair, share.

3 What kind of world would it be if God changed the laws of nature sometimes and not others? What problems would this present for religious people (or anyone actually)?

4 'If God is omnipotent, he could bring his own existence to an end.' What do you think about this? Would a religious person agree, do you think?

5 How well do you think Sources 1 and 2 challenge Hume's views about miracles?

Source 3

'Hume's biggest problem was that his argument was based on the idea that science can make comment about religion, and I don't think it can. Religious claims – like miracles – can't be scientifically investigated, especially if they happened in the past. But even modern miracles aren't able to be investigated by science because they are supernatural events and science deals only with natural events. And while we're on about it anyway, who says that the "laws of nature" are the same always and everywhere? Maybe there's a whole set of "laws of nature" which belong to the spiritual world and not the physical one. Bye bye, Hume.'

Source 4

'Hume based his theory on empirical evidence: things that can be measured and weighed up. This just needs you to set out the evidence for and against, then judge which is strongest and come to your conclusion. But miracles, and many other things in life, aren't like that. Imagine trying to weigh up the evidence for and against falling in love with someone; could you really investigate and form a conclusion on this based on empirical evidence? I wouldn't think so. Miracles can't be judged on empirical evidence because – by definition – they are well outside the normal range of empirical enquiry. Tough luck, Hume.'

Activity 2

1 Should science and religion avoid making claims about each other? What things might religion not be able to say about science (and vice-versa, of course)?

2 Try to weigh up the evidence for and against falling in love with someone. Is it difficult to do this?

3 Based on what you have learned in this section, should Hume have avoided saying anything about miracles? Has he caused more problems than he's solved?

Falling in love

The Large Hadron Collider at CERN, Switzerland

Source 5

'The biggest problem with Hume's argument is – Hume. You see Hume started with the idea that miracles are not likely and that the idea of God was questionable. He then matched up the "evidence" to fit in with the already existing set of beliefs that he had. Now that's not good science at all. Scientists don't just look for evidence that fits in with their theories; they look for any evidence, including evidence which goes against their theories. That's the point. Science moves on by rejecting old theories and replacing them with new, based on the evidence. Hume started with his beliefs, found his "evidence" and then finished with the same beliefs he started with, and round and round he went. That's enough of Hume then.'

Activity 3

1 Carry out some further research about Hume the man and then try to answer the question: 'Was Hume an atheist?'

2 Do you think scientists can put their own views to the side and deal with evidence only? Can scientists not have beliefs?

3 How might a scientist who also believes in miracles (they exist) explain miracles?

This section has given you the opportunity to explore a range of views on the question, 'Do miracles happen?'

If you're doing the N5 exam, you'll be asked to show what you have learned about **miracles in scripture** and **modern day miracles** as well as different views about how to interpret miracles (**literally** or **metaphorically**). You may be asked to write about religious or non-religious views.

You will also be expected to show that you can write about the strengths and weaknesses of the different views, and their impact on people's lives today.

Unlike a lot of assessments, the exam won't ask for specific viewpoints, so you will need to decide how to apply what you've learned.

Now try using what you've done in this section to answer the following exam-style questions.

Exam-style questions

1 '*It's important for people to think about whether miracles really happen.*' **Liz**
   Give **two** reasons why Liz might say this. **(4 KU)**

2 What sorts of things might someone describe as 'miraculous'? **(4 KU)**

3 Choose a religious viewpoint you have studied. Explain what it says about the importance of miracles. **(5 KU)**

4 Describe **two** scriptural miracles. **(6 KU)**

5 '*Miracles do **not** happen.*' What reasons might someone offer for this view? **(6 KU)**

6 What observations might lead someone to believe that miracles happen in the **modern** world? **(6 KU)**

7 Describe one non-religious response to belief in miracles. **(6 KU)**

8 (a) What is meant by a metaphorical interpretation of miracles? **(4 KU)**

   (b) Choose one miracle account you have studied. Explain what it might mean to someone who decided to interpret it metaphorically. **(6 KU)**

   (c) '*If you're religious, you need to take miracle stories literally.*' Would religious people agree with this statement? Give reasons for your answer. **(8 SKILLS)**

9 Explain how believing that miracles happen might affect someone in their daily life. **(4 SKILLS)**

10 '*What you believe about miracles is down to how you interpret the evidence.*'
    Do you agree? Give reasons for your answer. **(8 SKILLS)**

11 '*When it comes to understanding miracle stories, religious and non-religious people have nothing in common.*' Is this true? Give reasons for your answer. **(8 SKILLS)**

The origins of life

Source 1

We had the sky, up there, all speckled with stars, and we used to lay on our backs and look up at them, and discuss about whether they was made, or only just happened …

Mark Twain, *The Adventures of Huckleberry Finn*

Activity 1

1 Divide into two groups. Imagine it's you lying on a hilltop, gazing at the stars. (You'll need to rely on your imagination here, but you could do this for real if you get a clear night.)

2 Try to set aside your own views for now. Group 1 should list some reasons why someone might say the universe was 'made'. Group 2 should do the same for 'just happened'. Don't discuss your ideas yet.

3 Pair up with someone from the same group and compare your ideas. Tick any you both thought of, and choose your five strongest ideas.

4 Make groups of four with a pair from each side. Decide who is the spokesperson, and then argue for the view you've discussed. You can then ask each other questions and challenge any ideas you disagree with.

5 Discuss: What other questions might you ask yourself while you are stargazing? Do you think they are the sorts of questions that interest everyone? Who might have the best shot at providing an answer to them?

Source 2

You just have to wonder how it all got here, don't you? I mean, it's hard to ignore something as, well, as obvious as the universe. And if it's not here by accident, that must mean something, mustn't it?

Alistair

Source 3

I honestly don't care how the universe got here. Even if someone came up with a final answer, what does it have to do with me? There are plenty more important things for people to worry about.

Jon

Activity 2

1 If you were having a discussion with Alistair and Jon, what would you say?

- Does it really matter where it all came from?
- What would it mean if someone proved the universe wasn't an accident (or that it was)?
- Is it just daft to waste our time thinking about stuff like this? What might be more important?

Write your thoughts in thought bubbles, cut them out and stick them onto a big sheet of paper.

2 Spend some time reading each other's thoughts. If you change your mind, or you want to disagree with something, make another thought bubble and add it to the others.

3 Research: A man called Malunkyaputta approached the Buddha and asked him to explain the origin of the universe. Find out how Buddha answered him and then try rewriting the story, but with a modern setting. Imagine Buddha is taking part in this activity. Create a thought bubble for him and add it to the poster.

Source 4

A scientific story

Once upon a time, about 13.7 billion years ago, all of the stuff in our unimaginably big universe was concentrated into one unimaginably tiny particle. The particle was so small it was governed by the strange and unpredictable laws of quantum physics. It was a space–time singularity. There was no time and no space as we know it.

Somehow the singularity became unstable and it expanded with incredible force, blasting energy out in all directions and creating time and space as it went.

After about a second, the energy began to take the form of sub-atomic particles like protons, neutrons and electrons. These eventually came together to make simple elements like hydrogen and helium, the building blocks of matter.

It would be another billion years before matter began to come together in hot, glowing clumps; we call these stars.

Intense heat and pressure within collapsing stars fused hydrogen and helium to form the heavier elements that make up the universe today, things like carbon and iron.

By 10 billion years ago, billions of galaxies, containing billions of stars, had been formed, including our own Milky Way.

Then, about 4.6 billion years ago, a bright star in our galaxy ran out of fuel, became unstable, and exploded: a supernova. The dust and debris from the explosion was pulled into the gravity of big meteorites and came together to form the planets we see in our solar system today. These were then drawn into orbits around our Sun.

This means that everything in our solar system, from the most distant planets to the atoms that make up our bodies, is made of stardust.

Source 5

As far as the future of the expanding universe is concerned Einstein's equations do not provide a unique answer. They allow for several different solutions corresponding to different models of the universe. Some models predict the expansion will continue forever; according to others, it is slowing down and will eventually change into a contraction. These models describe an oscillating universe, expanding for billions of years, then contracting until its total mass has condensed into a small ball of matter, then expanding again, and so on without end.

Fritjof Capra, *The Tao of Physics*

Activity 3

1 Get a sheet of paper and a pencil and then close this book. One reader should give you the rest of the instructions (it's probably easiest if it's your teacher).

2 Reader: tell the story of the Big Bang slowly and clearly. Everyone else: on your own, listen and record what you're hearing, *but* (just to make it more interesting) you are *not* allowed to use any words, phrases or sentences. You *may* use pictures, symbols, initials and numbers.

3 Pair up and explain what you've recorded to your partner.

   ■ How did you decide what to put on the paper?
   ■ Identify any bits of your accounts that don't match.
   ■ Make corrections that would improve both of your accounts.

4 Give yourself a five-minute test. Without looking at your work, see what you can remember and write down an account of the Big Bang theory, but this time use words. Swap tests with someone else, and use Source 4 to mark it. You don't need to give it a mark or a grade, but try to write a really helpful comment.

5 *'Well, that's it then. We know how it all got here, and the mystery of our existence is solved!'* Discuss: Are our questions about the origin of the universe all answered? Is anything left unsolved? Write down any questions that you think the Big Bang theory does *not* answer. Does it raise additional questions? What does Fritjof Capra's reference to 'different models of the universe' show about answers in science?

6 Do you think religious people should see the Big Bang theory as a threat to their beliefs or might it support them?

Activity 4

Think and do!

1 Imagine you decide to make some tasty raisin bread. You mix your flour, water and yeast and after a good bit of kneading you add some raisins. Your dough looks pretty small to begin with, but as it proves in the warmth of the airing cupboard, it begins to expand, and the raisins all start moving away from each other. This is a nice illustration of the way galaxies fly apart from each other in the expanding universe (though considerably slower).

2 Get a balloon and draw dots all over the surface with a marker pen, then blow it up. Notice how the dots all move away from each other as the balloon inflates. The dots are a bit like the galaxies, which are still moving away from each other. Now let the air out of the balloon, and while you're enjoying the rude noises you can make with it, watch the dots moving closer together again.

3 Discuss how these illustrations correspond to the different ideas about the ultimate fate of the universe described in Source 5. One of these possibilities fits pretty neatly with traditional eastern cosmology. See if you can figure out which one, and why?

Source 1

A good deal of modern cosmology is, I think, reliable and trustworthy, because it talks about the moments in the universe's history when the physics that control that history is well known to us already, and which we have been able to investigate in a laboratory. It speaks of the behaviour of matter under conditions of energy and temperature and so on which are familiar to us and which are well understood. We can talk quite confidently and accurately about the history of the universe when it was say a second old, and certainly about the first three minutes of the universe's history. But cosmologists are bold people and they are not content with that.

John Polkinghorne, West Watson Lectures

Activity 1

1 John Polkinghorne is a mathematical physicist and a Christian priest. Without bringing religion into it just now, discuss what he is saying as a scientist about the Big Bang. Try to answer these questions:

- Does he believe it happened?
- What does he feel science can be sure about?
- What reasons does he give for his view?
- Does he think the theory leaves anything unexplained?
- What do you think he's getting at in the last sentence?

2 Do you think there are any questions about the origin of the universe that science will never be able to answer?

Source 2

What a lot of people don't realise is that the term 'Big Bang' (a term coined by the astronomer Fred Hoyle) was really poking fun at the notion of a universe expanding from a single point. Georges Henri Lemaître, a Belgian Catholic priest, physicist and astronomer was the first to suggest the idea; he called it 'the hypothesis of the primeval atom'. Einstein didn't like it at first, and said he was a nice enough guy, but his physics was dodgy, and Lemaître struggled to have his theory taken seriously by both the scientific community and the church. However, within twenty years the theory had become widely accepted, and shortly before he died in 1966 Lemaître heard about the discovery of Cosmic Microwave Background (CMB) radiation, what is now believed to be leftover heat from the moment of the Big Bang.

Georges Henri Lemaître

Source 3

Of course, Lemaître wasn't starting from scratch. There was already some exciting evidence that the universe was not a static place, that it was expanding. In 1929, the astronomer Edwin Hubble was studying the light coming from different galaxies. He noticed that the light from all the galaxies he observed was shifted towards the red end of the spectrum. Think about it like this. Light waves travelled across space from a distant galaxy, through Hubble's telescope, and into his eye. Now Hubble already knew that light waves that are being stretched have a lower frequency that makes them look red, and light waves that are being compressed have a higher frequency that makes them look blue. He reasoned that the galaxies must be moving away from us, and each other, just like the raisins in your imaginary raisin bread. This 'stretching out' of light waves as an object moves away from us is called red shift, or the Doppler effect.

The red shift

Edwin Hubble

Activity 2

1   Imagine you made a film of your raisin bread expanding as the yeast produces oxygen. You run the film backwards. What would you observe? If we could run a film of the expanding universe backwards, what would we expect to see? Would the recording keep going forever, or do you think it would stop?

2   See who can do a good impression of a Formula 1 racing car or the siren on a speeding fire engine as it passes. What happens to the pitch of the engine or the siren as it comes towards you, and then recedes (moves away from you)? How is the behaviour of the sound waves like the behaviour of the light waves observed by Hubble?

3   Your physics teacher is really impressed with your understanding of red shift and has asked you to design a poster for S1 pupils explaining how it works. Design and produce your poster using words and pictures. Can you think of any visual aids that could help your explanation further?

4   What would it have meant if all the galaxies had looked blue when Hubble observed them?

5   There seem to be a lot of religious people doing cosmology. Does this surprise you? Why might this branch of science be particularly interesting to religious believers?

6 Robert Wilson and Arno Penzias were radio astronomers who discovered one of the most important bits of evidence for the Big Bang – by accident. They won the Nobel Prize for their discovery. Find out what they discovered, how they did it and why it is so important. You might also want to look for some images of the map of the universe that was based on data taken from the COBE (Cosmic Background Explorer) satellite.

Source 4

Having found compelling evidence for an expanding universe, scientific attention has turned to what it's made of. Scientists reckon the early universe would have consisted of pure energy, and then, as it cooled, a kind of smooth 'soup' of sub-atomic particles. The physicists working at the Large Hadron Collider (LHC) at CERN in Geneva smash particles together so that they can get a glimpse of what the universe would have looked like in the first fraction of a second of its existence. Today we see a universe that's more like a stew made up of the bigger, lumpier elements shown on the Periodic Table (as well as any others that haven't been discovered yet). Complicated mathematical models have made predictions about how much there should be of the different elements (the ingredients in 'universe stew'), *if* the Big Bang is right, and guess what? It turns out they are absolutely spot on.

Source 5

Professor Peter Higgs of the University of Edinburgh and his Belgian colleague François Englert, proposed the existence of the Higgs Field (and its associated particle, the Higgs Boson) in 1964, but it was March 2013 before scientists working at the LHC spotted the first tantalising evidence that they had got the maths right. What had started out as some calculations made with paper and a pencil was now being observed and confirmed with real evidence in a $10 billion laboratory. For cosmologists it was an incredibly exciting achievement, because the Higgs was the missing piece in the working model of the universe (scientists call it the 'standard model'). It is important because it is needed to explain why everything in the universe has mass, including stars, planets and even us. One scientist has described it as 'the stuff that makes stuff stuff'. On hearing about the discovery Higgs said, 'It's very nice to be right sometimes.'

Professor Peter Higgs

Activity 3

1 See if you can find out what the main ingredients are for 'universe stew' and write down the recipe. To help you get started, you'll need around 90 per cent of it to be hydrogen.

2   Do an online search for ways people have tried to explain the Higgs for non-scientists, and then have a go at writing your own explanation in the form of a tweet. Display your tweets and compare them. Find out why the Higgs is important for the Big Bang theory.

3   Why spend $10 billion looking for information about what happened right after the Big Bang? Isn't the maths enough?

4   The Higgs Boson has been popularly called 'The God Particle'. Higgs doesn't like the name, and neither do a lot of religious people. Why do you think this is? Do discoveries about what the universe is made of get us any closer to knowing if it was 'made' or 'just happened'?

5   Because you are brilliant RMPS people, imagine you've been invited by your local primary school to teach P7 pupils about the Big Bang theory and the evidence for it. This means you will have to keep your explanations pretty simple. In groups, design some resources to make an interesting lesson, and an exercise to get the pupils involved and to check their understanding. Teach the rest of the class while they pretend to be in P7.

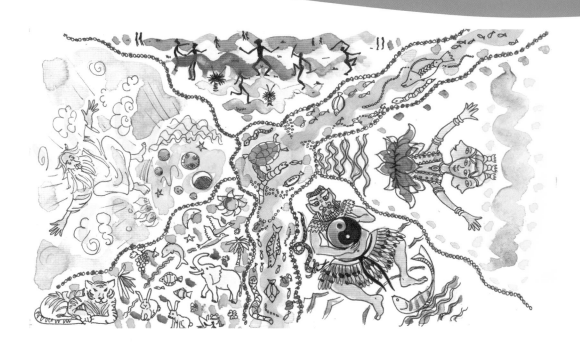

Source 1

Creation stories are clearly nonsense. I mean, are we honestly expected to believe that the universe emerged from the belly button of a goddess, or that God made it all in six days? Twenty-first-century people need twenty-first-century explanations, and the best people to give them are the scientists.

Sonia

Source 2

My creation story is not nonsense! For a start, it's from my holy scriptures, and that means it's the truth and that I can rely on it. If it was true when it was first written down, it's still true now.

Lora

Activity 1

1   Spend some time collecting different stories about the creation of the universe (don't include Genesis for now). Rewrite them in your own words, illustrate them, and bring them together into a small book. Produce a copy for each person in the class.

2   Make a list of the main similarities and differences between the stories. Discuss: Is it surprising that there are lots of different creation stories? Could they all be true? If not, should we just see them as nonsense? (You'll probably need to take some time here to discuss what 'truth' might mean when we're talking about these kinds of stories.)

3   Look back at the scientific 'story' in Chapter 23, Source 4. Can you see any points of agreement or disagreement between the Big Bang theory and the stories you have been exploring?

4. Find out what is meant by the word 'myth' in RMPS. Do you think seeing the creation stories as myths would change the views of the people in Sources 1 and 2?

5. Explore 'The Big Myth' project online. It looks at 25 creation myths from around the world and includes more activities you might want to try.

Source 3

Scene: Beside a river in ancient Babylon. A Jewish family living in exile relaxes together after the Sabbath meal. A young boy climbs onto his grandfather's knee and says, 'Grandpa, why do we rest from all our work on the Sabbath?'

'Well, because God told us to,' he replies.

'But why?'

'I think the best way to answer that question is with a story ...'

Activity 2

1. Pick up where Source 3 leaves off by getting a Bible and reading the first Jewish creation story in Genesis 1–2:4. Use the details of the story to create either a cartoon strip or a child's picture book. (Be careful; there is no mention of Adam and Eve in this one.)

2. Some thinkers believe this story originated in Babylon but was adopted by the Jews as a good way of putting across their beliefs. Get a big sheet of paper and write three headings: 'God', 'People' and 'The World.' Under each heading, list what the story is teaching. Discuss how much of the message of the story depends on it being historically true. You could tick the points that could be true whichever way you read it.

3. What is Source 3 suggesting about the possible purpose of this story? Does this affect the way it should be interpreted?

Source 4

'I think you need to be really careful about how you read the stories of creation in Genesis. For one thing, there are two stories, and they are quite different! The people who put them side by side knew very well the stories didn't agree, but they didn't seem to see that as a problem, or bother to try to match up the details. It seems likely that this is because they weren't trying to give a historical or scientific account of how the universe began. They were much more interested in the messages conveyed by the stories. Even in translation, there's loads about the first story to suggest that it was originally a poem or a song, maybe used in worship. The second story has a totally different style; a narrative, full of magical elements and symbolism. It's our job as readers to try to make sense of these poetic elements. If it's a scientific account we want, we need to look in science books, not Genesis!'

Source 5

'I think you need to be really careful about how you read the stories of creation in Genesis. Deciding everything is metaphorical is just another way of saying that you think it didn't really happen, and when you start doing that you're on a slippery slope! If you question what the Bible says about creation, you end up questioning what it says about things like Jesus' identity, and God's plan for the salvation of the world, and these things are just too important to mess about with. It's a basic belief for Christians that the Bible is God's word, and that means we can trust it completely. I for one think we should take it at face value. Besides, God is the all-powerful supreme being, so it would be no problem for him to make the world in six days.'

Activity 3

1 Imagine two people who have fallen madly in love. They spend most of the day gazing into the distance, sighing and writing soppy love poems. You get hold of some of the poems and discover that they have given very different accounts of their experience of love.

Discuss: Does this mean that only one of them has written meaningful poems? Would you expect two poets to see things in exactly the same way? If you decide to treat creation stories as a kind of poetic writing, does this affect what you expect from them, or how you interpret them? Try writing some poems about love or nature or something else you find really inspiring, and see how similar or different your poems are.

2 Get a 'write-on' copy of Genesis 1–2:4. Using different highlighters, see if you can identify some of the features of Hebrew poetry. You should look for:

- parallelism (saying the same thing in two or more different ways)
- chiastic structure (referring back and forward to similar or related ideas, e.g. day and night, sea and land)
- repetition.

3 Should we expect Genesis to give us a scientific account of the origin of the universe? If you read Genesis 1:1 and it said, 'In the beginning there was a space–time singularity. The singularity exploded, etc. ...' you should be suspicious. Why?

4 Is the story really about the origin of the universe as we know it today? Try drawing a picture of the universe as it was understood when Genesis 1 was written. Include the following features:

- flat Earth held up by pillars
- land and sea
- Earth covered with a dome
- water above the dome
- trap doors in the dome (to let the water through from time to time – rain!)
- Sun, Moon and stars in the sky (firmament)
- fire below the Earth.

Discuss whether this was a fair understanding at the time. Did it fit with what people observed?

5 Gather some information and statistics about the universe as we know it today. How big is it thought to be? How many galaxies? How many solar systems in the galaxies? How many stars? Could any of this have been known when Genesis was written? Has your work on this activity affected the way you think about the Genesis creation story?

6 Choose a creation story from one of the other big world religions. Find out what followers of the religion think it means. Do they take it literally? If not, what 'truth' might there be in it?

Source 1

Some creationist ideas

- Every word in the Bible was given directly by God.
- The Bible exists to give us the facts.
- The six days in Genesis are days of 24 hours.
- There's no real evidence for the Big Bang.
- The world was made between 6,000 and 10,000 years ago.
- Human reason is damaged, so we can't rely on ourselves to work out the 'truth'.
- If you don't take Genesis literally, you're saying God doesn't exist.
- If you don't take Genesis literally, you're saying human beings are not special.
- You can't believe in the Big Bang and creation.
- These atheist scientists are just trying to push God out of the picture.
- Creationism should be taught in science lessons as an equally valid explanation for the origin of the universe.

James Ussher, who estimated that the universe was completed by 23 October 4004 BCE

Source 2

Some compatibilist ideas

- God speaks to people through the Bible.
- The Bible exists to show the writers' thoughts about God.
- The six days in Genesis are a poetic device, and shouldn't be taken literally.
- There is loads of good evidence for the Big Bang.
- The Big Bang happened 13.7 billion years ago, and the Earth has been around for about 4.6 billion years.
- Humans have the ability to study the world and make sense of it.
- Reading Genesis metaphorically leaves room for God.
- Reading Genesis metaphorically shows humans are special.
- You can believe in the Big Bang and creation.
- The more we learn about the universe through science, the more we learn about God.
- Creationism should be studied in RMPS lessons as a religious belief about the origin of the universe.

Activity 1

1 Half the class should spend some time researching some key creationists. Find out what they believe about the origin of the universe and why, collect useful quotations, and use them to make a big collage. You should include any differences you find within creationism, e.g. do all creationists think the days in Genesis 1 were 24 hours long? The other half of the class should do the same for compatibilists.

2 Share your findings and do a compare and contrast exercise. Try to come up with a 'top five' reasons why the creationists and compatibilists don't agree.

3 Design a leaflet **or** write a letter to the education minister from a creationist point of view. In it you should explain why you think creationism should be studied in school alongside the Big Bang theory. Swap your work with someone and then write a

reply from the point of view of a person who thinks that creationism shouldn't be explored in school.

4 Discuss why someone might say that creationist ideas should be explored in RMPS. Could this be the view of a religious or a non-religious person, or both?

5 We've been looking at creationism in Christianity. Find out about creationism in one other big religion. Is it the view of all followers, or just some? Does the religion include compatibilists too? Are there arguments in this religion similar to the ones you've been looking at already in this activity?

Source 3

'I've spent my whole adult life doing science, and I'm convinced it's a reliable way of finding out about the universe. While I am happy to accept what science tells us about the processes in nature, I can't agree with those scientists who have concluded that these processes can only be the result of blind forces or chance. The more I study the nature of things, the more I'm drawn to the conclusion that there must be an intelligent designer behind it all. I don't need my religion or my holy book to tell me the universe was designed; the universe speaks for itself.'

Source 4

For life to exist on earth an abundant supply of carbon is needed … eminent mathematician and astronomer, Sir Fred Hoyle, found that for this to happen, the nuclear ground state energy levels have to be finely tuned with respect to each other. This phenomenon is called 'resonance'. If the variation were more than 1 per cent either way, the universe could not sustain life. Hoyle later confessed that nothing had shaken his atheism as much as this discovery. Even this degree of fine-tuning was enough to persuade him that it looked as if 'a super-intellect had monkeyed with physics as well as chemistry and biology', and that 'there are no blind forces in nature worth talking about'.

John Lennox, *God's Undertaker: Has Science Buried God?*

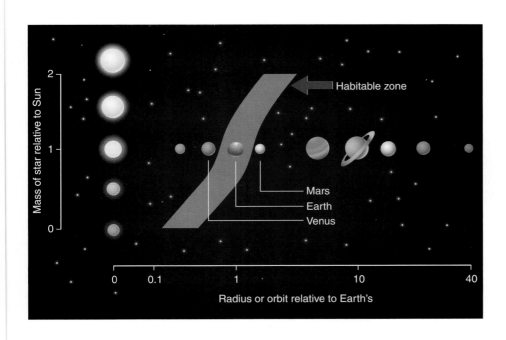

Activity 2

1. Intelligent design (ID) ideas are often seen as another kind of creationism. Is this the right label? Look a bit further into the claims of the ID movement and then use Sources 1 and 2 (on page 78) as a model for writing a new set of bullet points. (For now, focus on what they say about the origin of the **universe**.) How much overlap is there with creationism and compatibilism?

2. Is ID really about a 'God of the gaps'? Discuss what this means and why some people think it's a very risky approach.

3. Research the idea of the anthropic principle and 'fine-tuning', and gather examples of things science has shown are 'just right' for bringing about a universe with intelligent life in it. Do these observations make you feel '*lucky* to be here', or '*meant* to be here'?

4. 'The more I study the nature of things, the more I'm drawn to the conclusion there is no need for an intelligent designer.' (Atheist scientist)

   Atheist scientists and believers in ID are looking at the same evidence. Shouldn't they be reaching the same conclusion?

5. Some see intelligent design and the anthropic principle as modern-day versions of the classic teleological argument for the existence of God. Find out more about it in Section 1.

Source 5

'My reason for believing in a creator isn't so much about the nature of the universe, as its existence. The fact that it's here rather than not here is what interests me most. Common sense and observation tell us that things don't just appear out of nowhere. They are caused by other things, which are caused by other things, and we can trace long chains of causes back through time. Assuming it doesn't make sense to keep tracing the causes back forever, it's reasonable to think something must have started the whole process off. The 'something' would need to be uncaused (in other words, eternal) or else the chain would have to continue, and that just doesn't make sense. If an uncaused eternal being is needed to start everything off, we might as well call it God. Mind you, I'm not the first person to have had this thought. Plato and Aristotle thought the universe needed something to start it off, and in the Middle Ages St Thomas Aquinas said pretty much the same thing. It's called the cosmological argument because it's based on observation of the cosmos, but some prefer to call it the "first cause" argument, for reasons that should be obvious.'

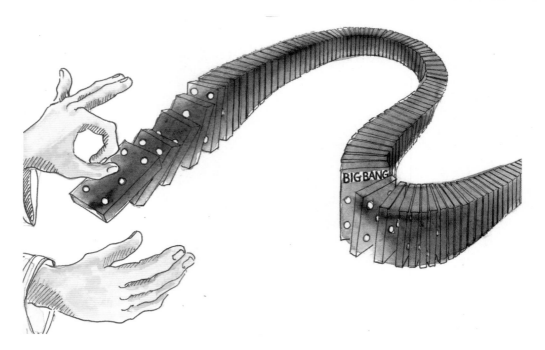

Activity 3

1 'But I know what caused the universe! It was the Big Bang!' How would the person who wrote Source 5 respond to this statement? Might the Big Bang theory even support the cosmological argument?

2 Do a quick survey of your maths teachers. Ask them if they think there's such a thing as 'actual infinity'; in other words, is infinity just a useful mathematical concept rather than something that is really possible. Did you get one answer? Why is this question important for people who believe in a first cause?

3 See if you can argue for the existence of God using only a piece of chalk. You'll need to think back through the chain of causes that led to the object you can hold in your hand. Here are some recent causes to get you started:

- The van from the stationery company delivered the chalk to school.
- The stationery company got the chalk from the factory where it was manufactured.
- The chalk factory got the chalk from a quarry (chalk is a naturally occurring compound called calcium carbonate).
- The chalk got into the quarry when ...

4 Is the kind of god needed by this explanation of the origin of the universe the kind of god most religious people believe in? Why might someone feel it falls short?

5 Discuss whether the cosmological argument would make sense to followers of the eastern religions.

6 Do you think it's possible to avoid saying something about God in a discussion about the origin of the universe?

Source 1

'I suppose myths and scientific explanations have a similar purpose, in that they are both ways in which human beings have tried to make sense of the existence of the cosmos. But that's where the similarity ends. Myths are primitive explanations from a time when many phenomena, which are now well understood by science, were believed to have supernatural origins: things like the movement of the stars in the heavens, or natural disasters. All of these stories have now been replaced by scientific explanations, and we know we can trust them because they are backed up with real evidence. These old stories just aren't relevant any more. People need to get their answers from a more reliable source.'

Source 2

'The appearance of 'fine-tuning' in the universe is just that: appearance. Certainly we are incredibly unlikely to be here, but when we say that conditions in the universe from the moment of the Big Bang have been 'just right' to bring about intelligent life, we're just describing how things happen to be, not how they were meant to be. It's like if you won the National Lottery. Sure, you'd feel really special and important, like it was meant to happen, but really it was just luck. I like to apply Occam's Razor when I'm thinking about fine-tuning. This is a principle in science and philosophy which says that, all things being equal, the simplest explanation for something is usually the right one. I for one find chance to be a far simpler explanation than some sort of all-powerful supreme being we can't see.'

Activity 1

1 Discuss what Source 1 is saying about the different explanations offered by creation myths and science. Do you agree that scientific explanations are a replacement for these stories?

2 Look back at some of the creation stories you found at the start of this section. If you accept the scientific explanation for the origin of the universe, do they have anything left to offer?

3 Use sticky notes or note cards to record some reasons why someone might say creation myths are no longer relevant. Do the same for the view that they are still meaningful. Which side of the argument do you find most persuasive? Take a class vote.

Source 3

In 1953, the American quantum physicist Hugh Everett III proposed the existence of parallel universes. He had a pretty hard time getting people to take the idea seriously at first – this was more science fiction than science – but it's an idea that has come to appeal to a number of scientists, among them the Astronomer Royal, Professor Sir Martin Rees. If it's true, it gets rid of the idea that our universe is very unlikely, and this means people should no longer feel a need to resort to belief in a creator God. The theory suggests that there are billions of different universes that all exist at the same time, and that even things that seem to have only a remote chance of happening are bound to happen somewhere. Our universe just happens to be the one where the conditions were right for human life to come about.

Galileo Galilei

Activity 2

1   Religious people are sometimes accused of having a geocentric view of the universe. Why might someone say this is the wrong way to see things? Find out what happened when Galileo Galilei suggested the Earth was not the centre of the solar system. How long did it take for his discovery to be officially accepted by the church?

2   Some cosmologists don't see the idea of parallel universes as 'scientific'. Why do you think this is? If it's not science, what is it?

3   Some thinkers have applied Occam's Razor to the idea of parallel universes. What do you think they concluded? Carry out an Internet search to find out.

4   Observation of 'fine-tuning' is often used by people who believe in a creator God. What does Source 1 show about this kind of 'evidence'? When it comes to the possible role of God in causing or designing the universe, do you think there could ever be conclusive evidence either way?

Source 4

The internationally acclaimed physicist Paul Davies is not religious, so it came as a surprise to some when he won the Templeton Prize for his contribution to 'affirming life's spiritual dimension'. Davies is intrigued by the orderliness of the universe and the scientific laws which have enabled intelligent life to come about. He believes these laws provide a full explanation for the Big Bang and everything that has happened since, but that this *doesn't* mean all of our questions are answered. Why these particular laws? Did they exist before the Big Bang? Where did they come from? In his prize address called *Physics and the Mind of God* he said, 'To me the true miracle of nature is to be found in the unswerving lawfulness of the cosmos, a lawfulness that permits complex order to emerge from chaos, life to emerge from inanimate matter, and consciousness to emerge from life, without the need for the occasional supernatural prod; a lawfulness that produces beings that not only ask great questions of existence, but who, through science and other methods of enquiry, are even beginning to find answers.'

Paul Davies

Activity 3

1   Davies talks about 'science and other methods of enquiry'(see Source 4, page 83). What other methods do you think he has in mind?

2   In groups, research Davies' views on science and belief further, especially when it comes to the origin and nature of the universe. You'll find the full script of his Templeton Prize address online at **www.firstthings.com**. Create a profile showing:

- some biographical information
- his views about the origin and nature of the universe
- his views about the relationship between science and faith
- what other scientists and religious thinkers think about his views.

3   Organise a class debate with the motion: 'When it comes to the origin of the universe, science and religion should stay out of each other's business.'

Source 5

Confirmation bias is a phenomenon well known to scientists, and it's important to consider it when we're thinking about 'evidence' for beliefs about things like the origin of the universe. It's the unavoidable human tendency to notice or give more weight to evidence that supports what we already think is true (and less weight to evidence that challenges our views). We might not be aware we are doing it, but it can have serious implications for the reliability of our conclusions. It's the reason why peer review and independent verification are such an important part of scientific method.

Activity 4

1   Do you think confirmation bias applies to religious beliefs too? What might an atheist and a believer in God notice that supports their views on the following statements?

- There is a creator God.
- The universe came about by chance.
- God is involved with the universe he has made.
- God does not intervene in the universe.

- The universe was designed.
- The universe was not designed.

2   How important is 'evidence' for people when it comes to belief? Does evidence always point in only one direction? Do you think people believe because of clever arguments, or are there other reasons?

3   Search online for Richard Dawkins' open letter to his daughter Juliet, called *Good and Bad Reasons for Believing*. Note down his main arguments. Do you agree with his conclusions? Write another letter to Juliet from the point of view of someone who believes in a creator God. Try to convince Juliet that you have good reasons for believing. (You could do an online search for religious responses to his letter too.)

4   Finally, get a sheet of A3 paper and write the heading 'Where did it all come from?' Draw a horizontal line across the full width of the paper and label one end 'Science' and the other end 'Faith'. Look back at the different views you have studied in this section. Plot them on the line to show where they are in the discussion and add a brief summary of the main ideas. Did you find it hard to decide where to put some of the views? Do you think we should see science and faith as opposites when it comes to questions about where it all came from?

Source 1

'Evolution is not a theory, it's a fact. Life on Earth has gone through so many different variations through time, each generation surviving or not because it can or cannot adapt to changes. It is sometimes called 'survival of the fittest' but many don't really understand what that means. The simple answer is that every time some species reproduces there's a chance of a genetic mutation happening. If this mutation is beneficial in some way then it increases the chance of the species surviving (in the right conditions) and passing on this beneficial mutation. Here's an example: Let's say that something caused oxygen levels in the atmosphere to fall drastically over a period of time. Now let's say that around the planet some people were born with a genetic mutation which gave them the ability to survive on much less oxygen than other people. Those people would survive, reproduce and, after a time, almost everyone on Earth would have that beneficial genetic mutation. That's evolution.'

A Galápagos finch

Source 2

Charles Darwin found different species of bird (each with a different beak size) on tiny islands in the Galápagos archipelago. At first he couldn't work out why this would happen; why would God create a different bird for each island? Eventually he matched this up with his evolutionary theory. There were different beak sizes on each island because there were different food sources on each island. Each different type of bird was best suited to a particular food type. For example, to crack open big hard seeds a big strong beak was needed so, over time, nature 'selected' the birds with such beaks on islands where that was the main food type; birds with other beaks died out. So, you see, Darwin showed that life evolved in steps, according to the environment in which it lived. The environment selected different species for different reasons at different times.

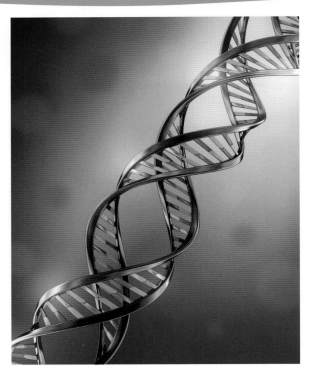

A DNA helix

1 What is the difference between a theory and a fact? Should evolution be taught in schools as a fact or as a theory?

2 What other possible genetic mutations can you think of which could be useful or advantageous?

3 DNA is the means by which genetic mutations are passed on. Find out about the structure of DNA and how mutations occur. You could create a presentation on your findings.

4 Illustrate the three different kinds of finch Darwin found, which got him questioning the biblical creation story. Explain how each one is adapted. You could do the same for the Galapagos tortoises.

5 Create your own class display about evolution.

Source 3

'Of course, some people would argue about how something as complex as an eye could evolve; what use is part of an eye after all? Well, actually, a lot of use in fact. The first 'eyes' would be no more than cells that could tell the difference perhaps between light and dark. This would be useful if something was about to eat you and blocked out the sunlight as it approached; you'd be able to take evasive action. Eventually, these dark–light receptors would, maybe over millions of years, be able to see different colours: helpful if your enemy was a particular colour (or your potential mate a different one!). Eventually, again over millions of years, those first 'eye cells' would have evolved throughout the generations into organs with the ability to see colour, depth, contrast, detect movement, tell friend from foe and so make life much more straightforward. Who knows, perhaps in a million years or so from now there will be human eyes that can see microscopic life (good for avoiding viruses) or radiation leaks or currently invisible harmful gases (good for avoiding harm) or X-ray vision (useful for doctors in diagnosing illness)?'

Source 4

'Evolution has no purpose; it is simple cause and effect. The environment changes and those organisms that can cope with the changes survive, and those that can't don't. This isn't cruel; it's just the way things are. It may not be all that positive for individuals – those who die out do so because they cannot adapt quickly enough – but it's often good for a species because it enables the species to survive. But, it all depends on how fast the environmental change is. The dinosaurs probably died out because of a very sudden environmental change which didn't give them enough time to adapt to it; but other species were already adapted to the changed environmental conditions and this allowed them to survive. Perhaps if the dinosaurs hadn't died out, there'd be no us. Perhaps one day the human species will die out and be replaced with something better suited to the new conditions.'

Activity 2

1 Using the model for the evolution of the eye in Source 3, think about how the other senses might have evolved through time.

2 There is no 'purpose' in evolutionary change. For some people, this is just the way things are, whereas others don't like it. What do you think? Discuss in class.

3 In groups, you will be given one of the following change scenarios. For your scenario, think about how humans would cope and if there are other species currently around that would cope much better than humans (and so have a better chance of surviving):

(a) average global temperatures rise by 30 degrees

(b) a meteor crash on Earth blocks out the Sun for five years

(c) bacteria and/or viruses kill off all the Earth's plant life

(d) climate change causes all land-masses on Earth to be covered in ice.

Source 5

'Imagine that one day a special hamster was born; one that could say a word or two in human language. Can you imagine how popular such a pet would be and how many would be bred? Imagine that with each of this amazing hamster's offspring the ability to speak just got stronger and stronger so that in just a few thousand years, all hamsters could have complex conversations. Now imagine that these hamsters started to ask why they had to spend all day in cages running in wheels. And after a time some hamster unions were set up and the issue of hamster rights became more important. Eventually, some hamsters became very militant and – to cut a long story short – this resulted in the human–hamster wars of the twenty-fourth century. Who would win? Would nature select the hamsters or the humans for survival?'

Activity 3

1 Think through the evolved hamster scenario. Who would win the human–hamster wars? Why? Could they reach agreement?

2 Imagine the early days of the talking hamsters. How would they be treated? What would happen to them? Would people welcome them or fear them? How might this affect the way humans treat other non-human species?

3 In species that reproduce relatively quickly, evolutionary change can be studied more easily. One example is the ordinary garden snail. Visit **www.evolutionmegalab.org** where you can carry out research into evolution in your own garden.

Scientific and philosophical support for evolution

Source 1

'Right, here we go. Throughout time there have been mass extinctions; this is where huge numbers of species have died out – completely. The dinosaurs are an obvious example, but there are others. You can find them in the fossil records. And there weren't just mass extinctions, there were also smaller-scale extinctions throughout time. If everything was created by God, then why did that happen? Did God have second thoughts about the things he'd made and decide to start over again? If so, then that's either a God who makes mistakes, or one who just changes his mind a lot; either way, that would be worrying. No, the simple answer to these extinctions is evolution. The species that died out couldn't adapt quickly enough to some change, and so were replaced by species who could survive the new conditions.'

The fossilised skeleton of a winged dinosaur

Source 2

Q Why is evolution true?
A Because of homologies.
Q What are homologies?
A Similarities between different species.
Q What's an example of one of these homologies?
A The bone structure of most mammals is pretty similar.
Q What does this tell us?
A That these similarities point to a common ancestor.
Q Why does this question creation by God?
A If God had created all life uniquely, why did he use the same basic design for so many things? Was he short of ideas?

Activity 1

1   Create your own web page which explains how fossil evidence supports evolution.

2   Think, pair, share. Why might a God who makes mistakes or changes his mind be worrying? Could a God be like that and not cause you worry?

3   Create your own class display about homologies and how these examples support evolution. You could choose one type of animal or plant to illustrate this or a range of plants or animals.

4   For each of the answers in Source 2, think of some more questions you might ask about this answer. (And then maybe some more answers to those questions. How far can you go?)

5   'The evidence in Sources 1 and 2 prove that evolution is a fact.' What do you think?

Source 3

Before we start let's hear it for those rare Australian beasts
Koala bears and kangaroos on leaves and grasses feast
There's possums and there's platypuses – should that be platypi?
The platypus likes to swim a lot, but possums stay quite dry
There's cassowary which are birds, a pretty fearsome sight
Saltwater crocs with pointy teeth who really want to bite
And tiny quolls with silky fur, all speckled with white spots
The quokka too – so very cute, on Rottnest Island trots
Don't forget the dingoes – dogs who live quite wildly there
But not as wild as devils (Tasmanian ones that is) who'd give you such a scare
There's emus who can run quite fast but sadly have no flight
And last of all there's echidna, a tiny spiky sight
'Where are they all?' you wonder
Down under.

An Australian cassowary

Source 4

'It's hard to see how anyone these days can deny evolution. We know that the Earth is around 4.5 billion years old. People who believe in the literal truth of the Bible say that it's around 6,000 years old (counting back the generations to Adam). If so, what was going on before that? We have fossil records which show how species have changed and evolved, and we can see it on a smaller scale in our own back gardens by counting the different types of banded snail we can find there. We can see that DNA structure is shared by living things and that changes to it led to changed species. We have evidence of the development of our own human species. Were Adam and Eve Australopithecus afarensis, Homo habilis or Neanderthal, or were they fully formed Homo sapiens like us, unchanged from the beginning? I would say that the evidence for evolution is just overwhelming and anyone who denies it is simply fooling themselves, and I don't know why they'd do that. Why would evolution being true mean that God isn't?'

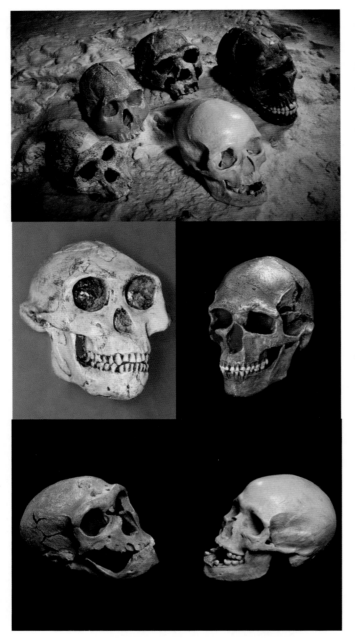

Hominids skulls: Homo habilis; Australopithecus afarensis; Homo sapien; Neanderthal

'OK, the science is complicated — can't deny that. So how can you get your head around the creation—evolution argument if you don't have a couple of PhDs in microbiologicalchemicophysics under your belt? Simple; it's about evidence against belief. In all aspects of our lives we work on the basis of evidence, and there is evidence for evolution — solid, unchallengeable evidence. Belief that God created life on Earth is based on belief, not evidence, and that's all there is to it. If it makes your life better to believe in creation instead of evolution, then that's up to you — but to do so, you need to completely ignore the hard evidence, and once you start ignoring evidence, your life is going to become very wacky.'

Activity 3

1 What examples are there in our lives where we trust only the evidence?

2 Where and when in our lives might we ignore the evidence?

3 Could there be any evidence supporting a belief that evolution is not true?

Activity 2

1 How does Source 3 (on page 89) support evolution? What other geographical examples are there of the same principle?

2 Write a similar piece of poetry for South America or the Galápagos Islands.

3 Do you agree that people who deny the truth of evolution are 'simply fooling themselves'?

Source 1

'I completely reject evolution. The Bible is 100 per cent true and it says that life on Earth was created by God in six days. You can't just choose which bits of the Bible to believe in and which you can ignore; it's all or nothing for me. So, how do I cope with things like the "fossil evidence" and the "extinction of the dinosaurs"? Simple; these are God's way of testing our faith. He put that "evidence" there to test our faith in his creation. And that business of us all having the same kinds of bones. Why would God not re-use an idea that he found worked well? What would be the point in coming up with completely new styles of creature all the time? My faith is in the Bible, so evolution is just wrong.'

Source 2

'I reject evolution too, but I like to think that my argument is a more scientific one. For me the big issue is how did the inorganic become the organic? What I mean is that there is a massive difference between a lifeless rock or chemical and a living thing. Now I know that evolution says that it took billions of years to change from non-living to living but I'm still not convinced that's possible, no matter how much time you've got. The jump from lifeless to life is just far too great for me; it needs some creative force to make it happen. I call that creative force God, but what that God is – that is a whole different question. I can see that some things in evolution do make scientific sense, but not the jump from lifeless to life. For me, that's the killer argument against evolution.'

Activity 1

1. Some Christians would say that Source 1 is the simplest and best way for a Christian to respond to evolution. What do you think?

2. Discuss in groups: Why would God want to test someone's faith?

3. Find out more about the inorganic–organic issue. Do you think this is a big challenge to evolution?

4. From what you learned in Chapter 28, is it possible for a Christian to accept evolution? What are the arguments for and against?

5. How does believing that the Bible is 100 per cent true help a Christian, and what possible problems might it cause him or her?

Source 3

'I don't reject evolution at all. I completely accept it. You just can't disagree with the evidence for it, and anyone who does really is clutching at straws. For me, they're not showing their faith at all, they're doing the opposite. They explain the evidence away, when you can be sure that if solid evidence was found for the existence of Adam and Eve, they'd be shouting a lot about that! So, does evolution mean that my belief that God is behind everything is wrong? No. Maybe evolution is the way God chose to start life off and let it take its course. I don't begin to understand why he would choose this method, but just because I don't understand it doesn't mean it didn't happen that way. So does my "belief" in evolution mean I don't believe in the Bible? No. The Bible is what it is and the creation stories in it are stories. It's not a science book.'

Source 4

'I'm kind of in the middle about evolution. I think some of the evidence is very strong and some is a lot less convincing. But then as a religious person, I find some bits of the Bible easier to accept than others. For me, nothing in life is black and white; it's all kind of grey. So I think that you can be a religious person who agrees with some of evolution but not all, and some of the Bible but not all. I think, too, that you can be a scientist who accepts all the evidence for evolution, but thinks that God is still in the picture somewhere. One doesn't need to cancel out the other; you can "believe" in both.'

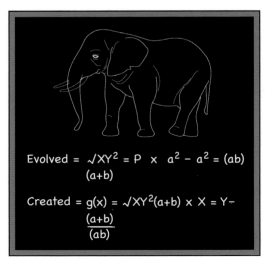

Evolved $= \sqrt{XY^2} = P \times a^2 - a^2 = \dfrac{(ab)}{(a+b)}$

Created $= g(x) = \dfrac{\sqrt{XY^2}(a+b) \times X = Y - \dfrac{(a+b)}{(ab)}}{}$

Activity 2

1 What kind of evidence would be needed to prove that Adam and Eve existed? Could this ever be agreed? How would scientists and religious people respond to this proof?

2 What other stories in the Bible could be seen as 'just stories'? Is rejecting that they are true a Christian not showing faith?

3 Discuss: Can a Christian believe in evolution?

Source 5

'As a Christian, I think we simply have to end this creation–evolution debate now. Most ordinary people like me really don't give a scooby about the science, and it's far too easy for people who support evolution or one or other of the versions of creationism to bamboozle us with stuff that we just can't get our heads around. Besides, and for me this is the most important bit, let's say that tomorrow, beyond all reasonable doubt, evolution or creationism were proved to be true in a way that no one could possibly deny. How would the world change; how would any of us change? My faith doesn't depend on the truth of creation or the truth of evolution; it's much more than that. So let's discuss what really matters – poverty, injustice, hatred, inequality – and how we put these right, no matter what you think of this tired old creation–evolution "debate".'

Activity 3

1 What are your views and the views of others in your class about Source 5?

2 What are the different versions of creationism? Why do you think there is such heated debate between creationists and those who support evolution? Do you think children should be discussing the creationism–evolution debate in schools? Is there an age when it's OK to do that and an age when it's not?

3 Make up a set of cards with statements that would be made by a creationist or a supporter of evolution (or someone who accepts both). See who can go through these cards most quickly and allocate them under the right headings.

Source 1

'God created Adam in his own image. So humanity shares something of God's nature. God then created Eve as Adam's mate. They lived in a perfect garden with only one real rule: not to eat from a particular tree. But they did and so sin entered the world because they tried to make themselves gods by their disobedience. For this they were punished and made to struggle for survival. This is what the Bible says and this is what I believe. I don't think it's "just a story". I think it's true. Who can say that it isn't? Who was there to see it except God and Adam and Eve? Why would it be in the Bible if God wanted us to ignore it? None of that would make any sense, so for me, the simplest and most obvious thing to do is to believe it. So I do.'

Source 2

'I too believe that there was an Adam and an Eve, and a garden and a snake and all that, but I think you have to be sensible about it all. Adam and Eve were not the very first two humans; they were two of the very first humans, and there's a difference. It is quite possible that life on Earth began in some way that I couldn't even begin to explain, but neither can the theory of evolution to be honest. Adam and Eve were just two of the population and their story is true, but it reflects all humanity. For me, what is behind it is my belief that the origins of human life are to be found in God. You see, I think there's something special about human life which separates it from all other living things, some kind of essence that no other life-form shares on this planet. That is because behind the creation of humanity is a creator, not a blind process of evolution.'

Activity 1

1 On the class board, write up the phrase 'Adam was made in God's image'. Now add sticky notes to this with views about what this phrase might mean.

2 When people are told not to do something, it makes them even more likely to want to do it. Is this true? Why? What makes people like this? Discuss these questions in groups.

3 In what ways are humans similar to other living things on Earth and in what ways are they different? Do you think any of these differences mean that human origins are different from the origins of any other life on Earth?

4 Some people think that being created by God gives life more meaning. What do you think they mean? Do you agree?

5 Create your own rhyming A to Z of Genesis Chapter 2, on the creation of human life. For example: A is for Adam, formed from the ground; B is for Bible, where the story can be found; C is for creation, at the hand of God; D is for the devil, now why he's there, that's odd ...

Source 3

'Yes, it is possible to completely accept evolution and also to completely accept that God was behind it all. Evolution is the technique God used to create life on Earth, including us. The Adam and Eve story is a myth: a story with meaning. Its meaning is about the fact that God made life and that his relationship with the life he created is not a simple one. So you see, I don't have to get into complicated arguments about the science of evolution and whether this matches up with creation; I simply believe that God created life on Earth and I need no evidence for that. That's why my faith is exactly that: a faith.'

Source 4

'I am a creation scientist – some call me a creationist – which is someone who believes that there is hard science supporting my belief that God created human life. I won't start trying to explain it because it's very complex (just like evolution). It's funny how some scientists say that young people should not hear about creationism because they are too young to understand it, but that they're not too young to be told about evolution! I think that for every part of the theory of evolution there is a scientific challenge to it. And I think that it will be proven to be wrong using science, not just belief. I also think that there is scientific proof for creation of life on Earth by God; but as I say, look into it for yourself.'

The Creationist Museum in the US has displays of humans and dinosaurs living in the same era

Activity 2

1   In groups, work through the story of Adam and Eve. Take a few lines of the story each and for each element of the story think about what this part might mean (if it is not literally true, that is). Put all your meanings together. Is there a clear, underlying meaning?

2   Who in a school should decide whether creationists or those who support evolution should be invited in to school, and how should they conduct themselves when in school? What should this person take into account and what factors should they consider before they invite such speakers in?

3   The creation science/creationist view is packed with complex science. Search 'creation science/creationism' on the Internet and make a summary of the kinds of evidence used to support their views.

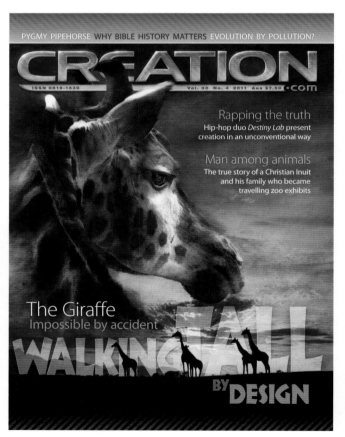

A creationist publication

Source 5

'I'm a Christian. I don't believe that the Bible is literally true; if it is, then that causes more problems than it solves. I don't believe that Adam and Eve were real people; if they were, then God's way of dealing with them isn't something that makes any sense to me. I don't believe that God created the universe in six days; there's plenty of evidence to show that this makes no sense. I don't believe that everyone is born a sinner because of the choice of one man eating one apple; if so, then that isn't the kind of God I'd want anything to do with. So what do I believe? That God made the universe. How? Who knows and who cares? That God brought about human life on Earth. Why? Who knows and who cares? That God is behind it all and knows about me and cares. Why we are still having these "arguments" about creation and evolution in the twenty-first century beats me.'

Activity 3

1 Have a look at some typical bible stories. In what way could each one 'cause more problems than it solves'? For example, Adam and Eve's son's wife.

2 Should religious people spend their time defending their faith against evolution? Do they need to? Should they be doing other things instead?

3 From what you have studied so far, do you think someone can be religious and also accept evolution?

The origins of human life: scientific and philosophical responses

Source 1

'A scientist simply has to reject the Bible's creation story. Our evidence of the development of early primates into the Homo sapiens we are today is just too strong. I don't even need to waste my time explaining the science; it's just too obviously accurate. There's no real point in me criticising the bible story because it isn't scientific, so what can I say about it? The fact that people still believe it is literally true just doesn't make any sense to me at all. They've buried their heads in the sand and are refusing to face up to reality. Besides, there are hundreds of different creation stories around the world; why should the Bible's be any truer than any other? No, it's a story from its time and place – nothing more.'

Source 2

'Creation science? Creation science! Seriously? It's an oxymoron. Like "act naturally". You look at these creation science websites and they are filled with what looks like science. They are written by people with proper scientific qualifications. They look like science, but they're not. Scientists start with theories and look for evidence to support or reject those theories. The "creation scientists" look only for the evidence that supports their theory, and they turn a blind eye to anything that might challenge it. Why don't they just save themselves a lot of time and say "I believe in creation" and leave it at that? How much time must these people waste on trying to find "evidence" to back up their ideas. I'm not saying some of them are not talented scientists, so please, they should use their talents to make progress in real science.'

The Hindu 'golden egg' creation story

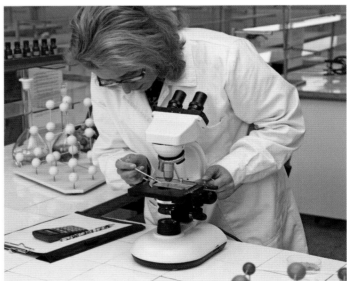

Activity 1

1 What other creation stories are there in world? Find out and display them. Does the range of creation stories make the Bible creation story more likely to be false?

2 Make your own timeline of the development of the human species.

3 Do you agree that creation scientists ignore evidence that goes against their theory? Do any other scientists do this? (This might be a good item to discuss with your science teachers.)

4 Some say that science and religion should stick to their own areas of expertise. What do you think these are? Create a diagram where you identify these and show any areas where you think they might overlap.

5 Have a debate in your class based on the motion 'This house believes that the creation–evolution debate should be brought to an end'.

Source 3

'Even if you don't understand a single word of the scientific arguments for and against the origins of human life – and I quite honestly don't – you can still reach a conclusion based on philosophical thinking without any science, so here goes.

- Science depends on empirical evidence (real hard, observable facts) to show that things are true.
- No one can turn the clock back and go back to witness the first appearance of human life on Earth (i.e. gather empirical evidence).
- Therefore there is no empirical evidence to support or reject any theory of the origins of human life.
- Therefore science cannot answer the question "How did human life begin?"
- Therefore your guess is as good as mine.'

Source 4

'Why do humans seem to have this need for either/or? It has to be this, and if it is not this, then it must be that. In behavioural sciences there is a debate called the "nature–nurture" debate. Scientists used to argue fiercely about which one made a bigger contribution to our behaviour. Now, of course, they see that both do – in complex and interacting ways – and they call it the "interactionist" approach. They're not opposites, they complement each other. Now what about creation and evolution? Is it just possible that they are not opposites, that instead they are both true? In the future might we talk about "interactionist evolutionary-creationism"? Now there's a thought.'

Activity 2

1 What are your views on Source 4? How do you think a scientist and a religious person might respond to it?

2 What would count as evidence that you could not ignore that would prove evolution or creation? Would we accept this evidence? Would we recognise it?

3 Is the science of 'interactionist evolutionary-creationism' possible? What would it look like?

'Let me sum it all up for you. The evidence for evolution is complicated and incomplete. The evidence against evolution is complicated and incomplete. The argument about what does and doesn't count as evidence for or against evolution is complicated and incomplete. The evidence for creationism is complicated and incomplete. The evidence against creationism is complicated and incomplete. The argument about what does and doesn't count as evidence for or against creationism is complicated and incomplete. Getting it? The whole issue is complicated and incomplete. So now, there are two things you can do. The first is carry on having these arguments, knowing that they will probably always be complicated and incomplete. The second is let them be and get on with living your life. Your choice.'

Activity 3

1   What choice have you made about the creation–evolution debate? Why have you made this choice and how does it differ from the choice made by others?

2   Create your own summary of the arguments for and against creation and evolution based on your study in this area. You could do this in the form of a song or a poem or in some other way.

3   Most of what you have examined so far is linked to the Jewish/Muslim/Christian creation–evolution debate. What about other religions? How do they respond to the creation–evolution debate? Do they deal with it at all?

This section has given you the opportunity to explore a range of views on the question, 'What are the origins of life?'

If you're doing the N5 exam, you'll be asked to show that you understand ideas about **God's role as creator,** as well as different views about how to interpret creation stories (**literally** or **metaphorically**). You may be asked to write about the **Big Bang** or **evolution,** as well as religious or non-religious views about these theories.

You will also be expected to show that you can explain the strengths and weaknesses of the different views, and their impact on people's lives today.

Unlike a lot of assessments, the exam won't ask for specific viewpoints, so you will need to decide how to apply what you've learned.

Now try using what you've done in this section to answer the following exam-style questions.

Exam-style questions

1 *'It's important for me to have an explanation for the origin of life.'* **Alex**
   Give **two** reasons why Alex might say this.   (4 KU)

2 What reasons might someone give for believing the universe was made by God?   (6 KU)

3 Explain how belief in a creator could affect a person in their daily life.   (4 SKILLS)

4 Choose a religious viewpoint you have studied. Explain what it says about the origin of the universe.   (5 KU)

5 Describe the theory of evolution.   (5 KU)

6 Compare two religious responses to evolutionary theory.   (8 SKILLS)

7 (a) Give the main points of the Big Bang theory.   (4 KU)

   (b) *'The Big Bang theory gives a complete explanation for the existence of the universe.'* Do you agree? Give reasons for your answer.   (8 SKILLS)

8 (a) Explain what is meant by a 'literal interpretation' of creation stories.   (4 KU)

   (b) Explain possible advantages and disadvantages of reading creation stories metaphorically.   (8 SKILLS)

9 *'The universe can't be an accident!'* Do you agree? Give reasons for your answer.   (8 SKILLS)

10 Explain some possible consequences of believing that life and the universe are **not** designed.   (4 SKILLS)

11 *'When it comes to understanding the origin of life, religious and non-religious people will never agree.'* Is this true? Give reasons for your answer.   (8 SKILLS)

The problem of evil and suffering

The world (… and your experience as an inhabitant and observer of it)

Activity 1

1 You are a kindly and intelligent alien from the planet Durdle-Durdle. You've been on an undercover mission for several years now, observing the third planet from a fairly insignificant star. You've visited lots of countries on all seven continents, and met loads of interesting people. You've also watched a lot of television. It's now time to report back to the Supreme Commander. What's life like for the creatures living on planet Earth? Should the Durdles plan a visit, or move quickly on to the next inhabited world? Write your mission report to the Supreme Commander (that's your teacher).

2 Share your conclusions with each other. What's life like for Earthlings? Is it wonderful? Is it awful? Is it both? Is it fair? If you reached different conclusions, try to figure out why. Display your reports for other people to read.

3 If you could give the world a make-over, what would you change? Are there some things about life on Earth that we just have to accept?

4 Spend some time online looking at interviews with astronauts recalling what it was like seeing Earth from space and how it affected their perspective. Canadian astronaut Chris Hadfield's tweets from space are a good place to start.

Activity 2

1 What do we mean by the word 'suffering'? What comes into your head when you hear it? You can use sticky notes, show-me boards or some scrap paper to write down single words (say up to five). Take some time to display them and explain your choices to each other. Then do the same thing for the word 'evil'.

2 These two ideas often appear together as aspects of the same problem, so how are they connected? Discuss: Are they really just different words for the same thing? Could there be suffering without evil? Could there be evil without suffering? Is there any such thing as evil? Agree on working definitions for each, and write them down.

3 Spend some time researching what religious people mean by 'suffering' and 'evil'. What different aspects of life would they include? Are any of them particular to the religion you are investigating? Are there any that wouldn't mean anything to a non-religious person?

Source 2

Your teacher will need to help you find this source: a selection of this week's newspapers (so it's up to date, and so you can chop it up with scissors).

Activity 3

1 You'll need scissors, glue, poster paper and some marker pens. In groups, spend some time identifying examples of suffering in the newspapers and cut them out. Don't stick anything down yet. Maybe share examples of suffering that you are aware of in your own life or the life of someone you know. You can write them on small pieces of paper. (You don't need to use names.)

2   Now discuss the different *kinds* of suffering you've identified. Try to arrange them into categories; you should decide as a group how to do it. Give the categories headings, and then stick your examples onto the poster paper and display them for the rest of the class to see.

3   Come back together as a class and discuss how you decided to categorise the examples of suffering you found. Did everyone go about it in the same way? Is all suffering the same in terms of scale, impact, avoidability, fairness, cause? Do people maybe use the word 'suffering' to mean different things?

Source 3

'I think human beings have to take most of the blame for suffering. Fair enough, sometimes we don't set out to hurt others – accidents can happen – but so much of the suffering we see around us is a result of people's stupid selfishness and cruelty. I sometimes think the world would be better off without people in it!'

Source 4

'We can't blame people for everything that's wrong with the world. For one thing people suffer in natural disasters, and we can really only blame the laws of physics for them. And in any case, it's at times of terrible suffering that we get to see how selfless and kind people can be.'

Activity 4

Analyse suffering a bit further by making a Venn diagram (named after a man called John Venn, who invented them). They're used in maths to organise information into groups or 'sets'.

1   Start by getting a sheet of A3 paper. Draw two large circles which overlap (the whole page is 'the universe', i.e. all the examples you are trying to sort, and the bit where they cross over is called the intersection).

2   Write 'Suffering and Evil' at the top of the page and use the labels 'Caused by nature', and 'Caused by humans' for the two sets. Your Venn diagram should look something like this:

3   Now look back at the posters you made for Activity 3. Use the examples you've identified to fill in your Venn diagram. Put anything that has a *combination* of natural and human causes in the intersection. If any of the examples don't fit into the circles, put them outside.

4   **Discuss:** What conclusions can you reach from this bit of analysis? Are the two sets enough to cover all your examples? Should there be other sets too? How would you want to label them?

5   Some thinkers have a different way of categorising the sources of suffering in the world. They prefer to talk about 'natural evil' and 'moral evil'. Discuss what these labels are suggesting, and whether you find them more or less helpful than 'nature' and 'human' when you are thinking about the sources of suffering and pain in the world.

Activity 5

Do this activity in groups. You'll need a large sheet of paper and some marker pens.

1 In the middle of the page write 'QUESTIONS ABOUT SUFFERING'.

2 Discuss the questions that are raised for people when they are suffering, or when they see others suffering, and use them to make a spider diagram. Would religious people find themselves asking different questions from non-religious people? Highlight the questions that only arise for religious people. Share your ideas with other groups before moving on.

3 Now discuss some different responses people could give to the questions. Aim to add at least two different possible responses to your poster for each question.

4 After sharing your ideas, get a sheet of A4 paper and make a personal copy to keep. You could try turning your poster over and doing as much of your personal diagram as you can from memory.

Source 1

Everyone knows what God is meant to be like.
God is:

- eternal
- formless
- the creator of everything that exists
- all-knowing (omniscient)
- all-powerful (omnipotent)
- in control of everything
- interventionist (gets involved and acts in the world)
- transcendent (totally beyond us)
- immanent (right here with us)
- just (fair)
- loving
- compassionate.

Activity 1

1 Look at each of the characteristics of God listed in Source 1. Discuss what you think each of them means and decide whether there are any you should add to the list (or any you might want to remove).

2 In groups, think about whether the existence of evil and suffering challenges any of these ideas about God. Use sticky notes or note cards to record your views. For example, you might want to say 'Suffering means God can't be just because ...'. If you think any of these characteristics can't be true about God, does that mean he can't exist? If not, what does it mean?

3 After sharing your views, see if you can come up with some ways in which religious people might respond to the statements you've written down. Maybe change the colour of your pen and continue with '... however a religious person might say ...'.

Source 2

Is God willing to prevent evil,
but not able?
Then He is not omnipotent.

Is He able but not willing?
Then He is malevolent.

Is he both able and willing?
Then whence cometh evil?

Is He neither able nor willing?
Then why call him God?

Epicurus (341–270 BCE)

Epicurus

Source 3

I grew up believing in God. I had no reason to doubt he was real, and I was used to thanking him for all the good things in my life. But then my family had a terrible year; first with redundancy and money problems, and then a lot of illness. Then when we lost my dad to cancer I began to question everything I had been told. I'm not sure what to believe any more. Maybe the atheists are right when they say God doesn't exist. Or maybe there is a God, but I've just got him all wrong.

John

Activity 2

1 Discuss what Epicurus is saying in Source 2 (on page 105). What different options does he think people have when it comes to belief about God, and what are his reasons?

2 What sorts of things might have led John in Source 3 (also on page 105) to consider the possibility that God just doesn't exist? What might have led him to wonder if he had just 'got him all wrong'? If John decides to continue believing in God, how might he want to change his understanding of what God is like?

3 Get a copy of the Christian hymn 'All things bright and beautiful' (see Chapter 8) and Monty Python's parody 'All things dull and ugly'. Do you think the Pythons were questioning the *existence* or the *nature* of God? Do religious people have to accept that God made the rotten things about the world as well as the good things?

4 *'Whether God causes or allows suffering, I still believe it is part of his good plan for the world.'* Could suffering and evil really be part of a 'good plan'? Discuss why many religious people would agree with this statement. Split the class into two groups and each consider one of the following possibilities:

   (a) God *causes* suffering for a good reason.

   (b) God doesn't cause suffering, but he *allows* it for a good reason.

   What 'good reasons' could God have in these two statements?

Source 4

'Omnipotence is one of the first things people think of when they are describing God, but what would it mean to be truly omnipotent? I mean, wouldn't being all-powerful mean that God could do absolutely anything you can think of, like make $2 + 2 = 5$, or a four-sided triangle? Maybe it's better to say that God can do anything that makes sense or is possible. After all, something doesn't stop being nonsense because you bring God into it.'

Activity 3

1 Try to think of some other examples of things that would be nonsense if we said God could do them. Include things that would mean having to go against his own nature; for example, could God go running until he ran out of breath, or tickle his own nose until he sneezed?

2 Research what St Thomas Aquinas, Rene Descartes and C.S. Lewis had to say about God's omnipotence. Design a leaflet explaining their ideas.

3 Let's assume Epicurus was right and God would have the power to put a stop to all the evil and suffering in the world. Do you agree that only a malevolent (cruel, nasty, spiteful) God would choose to do nothing?

Source 5

'For me, a really important part of God's nature is that he wants to give his creatures (and the universe for that matter) the gift of freedom. For us humans this means freedom to choose how to behave, with all of the accompanying risk. For the universe it's the freedom to evolve naturally according to the laws of physics (what the Christian physicist John Polkinghorne calls "free process"). Suffering and evil is simply the price we have to pay for having this gift, but to be honest, I can't think of a better alternative.'

Activity 4

1 In groups, discuss the pros and cons of bringing the idea of 'the gift of freedom' into a discussion about God's role in suffering and evil. Talk about human freedom, but also freedom for the universe to follow the laws of physics.

2 If you were out walking and you tripped over a paving stone, would it make sense for God to turn the pavement into a big fluffy pillow just before your face hit the ground? How else would God have to interfere with nature if he wanted to stop suffering? Could this kind of interference be seen as God going against his own nature?

3 Get into pairs. One person should prepare to argue for one minute that 'God should stick to a non-interference policy', while the other should get ready to argue that 'God needs to get more involved!' Discuss in your pairs, then take a whole class vote to see which statement has most support.

4 Do you think freedom is enough to let God off the hook for the existence of suffering and evil? Might there be a 'better alternative'? (We'll deal with this important idea in more detail in the next chapter.)

5 The seventeenth century saw a rise in the popularity of an alternative view about God called Deism. Carry out an Internet search to identify the main features of Deism (**www.moderndeist.org/f-a-q** is good for information on a current form). Might Deism offer a helpful alternative to more traditional views about God? Why might some religious people find it unsatisfactory?

Activity 5

What do the religions say about God?

1 In groups, research what at least two of the main world religions say about the nature of God. You could focus on the ones you want to study in more depth later in your RMPS course.

You can include ideas from holy scriptures, songs and poetry, teachers and followers, and images (if the religion uses them). If you find that the religion seems to be saying different or even contradictory things, make a note of that too.

2 Using the information you've gathered, prepare a five-minute lesson for the rest of the class. Explain what you've found out, and maybe give your learners a summary of the main points. Devise an exercise or task to check their understanding.

3 Do the views you have researched have anything in common? Do the religions have a consistent view on the nature of God, or did you get different messages? If God is real, should we be surprised that there are different ideas about what he/she/it is like?

Source 1

'Even if we're not sure what's the right thing to do, we have religion to guide us, and in the end it's up to us to choose whether or not to follow it. No one forces us into doing anything. What we do is down to personal choice, and personal choice is possible because we humans have this thing called "free will". Of course, the flip side of having free will is that we also have to take responsibility for what we decide to do, and this means accepting that you can't blame anyone or anything else for your choices. Only you can take the blame, or the credit, for your behaviour.'

Source 2

'It's hardly controversial to say human beings aren't free; it's just stating the obvious, isn't it? I mean, we're limited by all sorts of things. For one thing, our physical bodies put a lot of limits on us: no matter how much we might want to be able to fly or to breathe under water, we just don't have that capability as humans. It's exactly the same when it comes to our moral choices. There are loads of things that limit our freedom, things we have no control over. Sometimes it's ok to say, "It's not my fault".'

Activity 1

1   Discuss why free will and responsibility are important ideas for religious people. Why might they be especially important in a discussion about suffering and evil?

2   Draw a horizontal line on a sheet of paper and label one end 'Totally free' and the other end 'Not free at all'. Put an X on the line to show how free you think you are. Pair up and compare your answers. How did you decide where to put the X? Does your decision raise any problems for how religious people think about other people, God and the world?

3   'Free will means the ability a person has to make completely free choices between real alternatives or possibilities.' How helpful do you find this definition? What might limit people's freedom to choose, and when do people have real choice?

4   Current estimates say there are around 250,000 child soldiers fighting in brutal conflicts in Africa. Sometimes the children have to kill or maim a member of their family as part of their initiation. Does it make sense to talk about these child soldiers as having free will and responsibility?

Child soldiers in Africa

5   Split into six groups; each group should take one of the big six world religions. Find out what each religion says about free will, including the things that make it hard for people to do the right thing. Report back to the rest of the class. See if you can condense the main points about each religion into about five key points and fit them onto one side of a record card.

Consider two people:

Joanne started drinking as a way of coping with stress. She found it helped her to relax after a hard day, but it wasn't long before she couldn't get to sleep without a drink. It didn't take long for her to realise that she was dependent on alcohol and needed help to give it up. She hasn't had a drink for three years now. 'I just have to take each day as it comes,' she says.

Adam's childhood was pretty chaotic. He didn't have many boundaries. He only seemed to get attention when he misbehaved, and that was usually a clip round the ear. By the time he got to secondary school he was regularly in trouble for getting into fights. He's just been charged with assault after punching a guy in the street. 'He nicked my parking space!' he says.

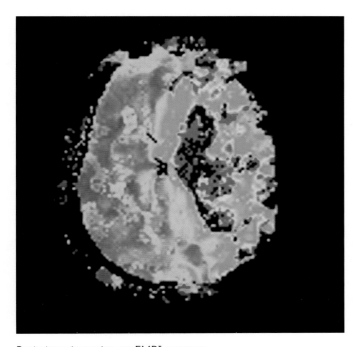

Brain imaging using an FMRI scanner

Activity 2

1   Do Joanne and Adam have as much free will and responsibility as anybody else? What if it was shown that there is a history of alcoholism in Joanne's family and that she has a genetic predisposition to addiction? What if some neurologists decided to take a look at Adam's brain in an FMRI scanner and discovered that the area of his brain that deals with primitive reactions is much more developed than the area that deals with rational thinking and relationships?

2   Think of some other examples of situations where making a good decision might be much harder for some people than others. Note down at least three and share them with the rest of the class.

3   Many countries allow defendants in criminal court to enter a plea of 'diminished responsibility'. Why do you think so many legal systems have adopted this option? You could discuss the trial of Anders Breivik who was charged with the murder of 77 people in a bombing and mass shooting in Oslo. The defence argued that he was mad, not bad, but the jury didn't agree.

'I'm a determinist! I believe free will isn't possible. We may feel as though we're making free choices, but we aren't really. This is because we are affected by lots of things that happen before we make the choice; we just aren't aware of them. Everything that happens, including every human thought, feeling or decision, is totally inevitable! Here's why:

- Stuff (matter) has to follow the laws of physics; it has no choice.
- Everything in the universe is made of stuff.
- Our bodies are part of the universe, so they are made of stuff.
- Our thoughts, feelings and emotions are just a result of stuff interacting with other stuff in our bodies (for example, hormones can make us feel happy or scared or in love, and thinking is just chemical and electrical signals between neurones in our brains).
- The stuff that makes our bodies has to follow the laws of physics too.
- This makes everything about us, including our thoughts and choices, completely predictable and determined by the laws of physics.'

'Either you believe people are just biological machines, or you accept that there must be more to human beings. For some the "more" is God's image, or the soul, or what the philosopher Immanuel Kant called "The Moral Self". Whatever label you decide to give it, it means recognising that there's a mysterious part of human beings that isn't material or measurable. We know it's real because we experience it every day of our lives. We reflect on the options before us, and we use our reason to make decisions. Sometimes we choose to act against our instinct, or to do something we'd rather not do (like homework!). This is what makes us different from the rest of the animal kingdom, and it's the reason why I think we can believe free will is real.'

Red, or green?

Activity 3

1 List five ways in which you have thought about different options and made a decision since you got up this morning. Did you decide to do anything you didn't really want to do? Is it reasonable to believe that when you decided to wear red underpants, or have Rice Krispies® for breakfast, that you couldn't possibly have made any other choice?

2 'Without free will there can be no moral responsibility.' Is this true? If humans can't be held responsible for their choices, can they still be held responsible for some kinds of suffering? If not, who or what has to get the blame? How might determinism cause problems for things like the criminal justice system?

3 The kind of determinism described in Source 4 (on page 109) sometimes gets the label 'scientific' or 'biological'. You'd be unlikely to find religious believers who accept it, but there's another kind of determinism that some do accept. It gets the label 'theological' and means that things are determined because of God.

Look back at the list of ideas about God given in Chapter 35 (see Source 1, page 105). Can you work out which ones might lead to the conclusion that people can't have free will?

4 *'God may already know everything I'm ever going to think or do, but that's just because he has a different perspective. I'm still able to make completely free choices.'* (Amy)

Is Amy just contradicting herself, or does God's 'perspective' make a difference when we're thinking about free will?

5 Finally, look back at where you put the X on the line in Activity 1. Do you want to move it now? Explain your decision to one or two other people.

Source 1

'I find it really hard to get my head round the part God plays in suffering. On the one hand, the Bible seems to point to a good God who is compassionate and caring, and who intervenes in the world to get his people out of trouble. But then I read some other stuff (especially in the Old Testament) and it seems like God doesn't think twice about destroying entire cities or striking down people who don't do what he wants. Maybe we just have to accept that we can never understand fully what God is doing, and that in the end he knows best.'

Source 2

About 2,500 years ago a story was written about a man called Job. Now everyone knew Job was a really good guy, but one day he found himself unexpectedly caught up in a sort of bet between God and Satan. You see, Satan was convinced that Job was only faithful to God because he had a great life, so God agreed to let Satan unleash horrible suffering on Job to prove that he would remain faithful, no matter what. Poor old Job: his children were killed, he lost everything he owned and he got a horrible disease which covered him in agonising sores. Even so, he remained faithful to God.

Activity 1

1   In groups, get a large sheet of paper and write the heading 'God and suffering'. Look up these Old Testament references (your teacher may want to give you some more) and create a poster or presentation showing what they are saying about the part God plays in suffering. Is it something God causes or allows? Does it have a purpose? Do people have any responsibility for the suffering described?

   - Genesis 38:7–10
   - Exodus 32:25–29
   - Numbers 15:32–38
   - 2 Samuel 12:14–18
   - 2 Kings 2:23–24
   - 2 Chronicles 21:13–19
   - Jeremiah 11:9–11
   - Amos 9:4

2   You're having lunch with some friends when one of them says she thinks that things like HIV, 9/11 or natural disasters could be a punishment from God. What would you say to her? How do you think she would defend her position? Try role-playing the conversation.

3   Job and three of his friends try to figure out what the real cause of his suffering is. Read Job 1. If you were studying this in English as a drama, you'd notice that the writer is using a nice bit of dramatic irony here. (If you don't already know what this means, find out!) What do we get to know about the reason for Job's suffering?

4   Read Job 38–42. Discuss God's answer to Job's complaint that his suffering is simply not fair. List the pros and cons of deciding to just accept that God's reasons for causing or allowing suffering are a mystery. Should God have told Job what we know from Chapter 1?

I believe what it says in Genesis. God made a perfect world with no pain or suffering or death. Then he made the first humans, Adam and Eve, and they were perfect too. Everything would have been just fine if they had only managed to follow the one rule he gave them. It was their inability to resist temptation that led them to eat the forbidden fruit, and now we're all paying the price for what they did.

Rosie

I believe what it says in Genesis too, but I don't think you can blame Adam and Eve. For one thing, I don't think they really existed. Adam and Eve are literary creations, invented to teach an important lesson about human beings. It shows that we aren't robots — we have free will — but we would all rather do our own thing than what God wants. In the end, this is bound to lead to suffering. I guess you could say we're all Adam and Eve.

Martin

Activity 2

1 Read the story of Adam and Eve in Genesis 2–3. Create a visual presentation showing how things were 'before' and 'after' they committed the first sin.

2 Why might Rosie think it's important to read the story as historical fact? What are the implications of reading the story literally? Think especially about how it would impact on other beliefs you would have about a) God, b) people, and c) the world.

3 Why might Martin think the stories shouldn't be read literally? What are the implications of seeing the story as a 'myth'? (You may need to check what we mean by the word 'myth' in RMPS.)

4 Is it possible for a story to be true without it being factual or historical? Here's a well-known one to discuss: 'The boy who cried wolf'. Can you come up with any other good examples?

5   What do you think Martin in Source 3 means when he says 'I guess you could say we're all Adam and Eve'?

6   Some people think the snake in the Adam and Eve story was really the devil in disguise. Based on your discussion about this story, do you think it could ever make sense for a Christian to say 'the devil made me do it'? The devil is involved in Job's suffering too. How might the idea of a *real* evil force in the form of the devil or demons raise questions for Christians when they are thinking about the nature of God?

7   Find out about St Augustine's Free Will Defence. Was he defending a belief in free will, or something else?

Source 4

Jesus was walking with his followers when he spotted a man sitting at the side of the road. The man had been blind from birth. His followers asked him, 'Is he blind because of his own sin or his parents' sin?'

'Their sin has nothing to do with it,' Jesus replied. 'He's blind so that God's power can be shown working in him.'

He spat on the ground to make some mud, pasted it on the man's eyes, and then told him to go and wash it off. The man did as he was told, and found he could see.

Adapted from John 9:2–4

Source 5

'As Christians I think we need to accept that there just isn't an easy answer to why people suffer, and Jesus certainly didn't seem to want to provide one. But when we read about how he was filled with compassion for suffering people, and how he stood and cried at the grave of a dear friend, we get a real sense that God doesn't see it as a good thing. What Jesus did show is that a lot of suffering is avoidable. Rather than trying to make sense of the mystery of suffering, I think we should ask what we can do about it, and Jesus' teaching and example is a good place to start.'

Activity 3

1   What reason does Jesus give for the man's suffering in Source 4? Do you think it would offer any comfort to people who are suffering?

2   In groups, spend some time researching what Jesus did when he came across suffering people. Look at his teaching too, such as the story of the Good Samaritan. For each example you find, give a modern-day example of how Christians could try to follow Jesus' example. Show what you've found in a poster entitled 'What would Jesus do?'

3   At the heart of Christianity is the idea that God became a human being, lived, suffered and died. How might this belief be helpful (or unhelpful) for Christians who are suffering?

4   'Suffering is never good, but good can come out of it.' Look at this list of ways in which Christians could say that suffering can have a good outcome.

- You become a more compassionate person.
- You get a chance to help others.
- It makes you stronger.
- You learn an important lesson.
- Others learn an important lesson.
- It brings people together.
- It strengthens your faith in God.
- It strengthens other people's faith in God.
- It helps you feel connected with Jesus.
- It lets you prove you trust God.

Choose one statement and decide whether or not you agree with it, then pair and share your reasons. Take the statement your partner spoke about and repeat the process, sharing with another. Keep sharing until you have heard and given a view about all of the statements.

5 *'People need to get the right perspective! This life is short and painful, but all of that is nothing compared with eternity in heaven.'* Get a Bible and read Romans 8:18–25. Discuss what the writer is saying in this passage. Do you think having a different perspective could help Christians who are faced with suffering and evil?

Create

Imagine a devastating earthquake has struck the town where you live. Many people have lost loved ones, their homes and livelihoods. You've been asked to give a religious 'Thought for the day' on local radio and you want to get across a Christian perspective on what has happened. Using your work on this section, write your script and perform it for the class. Finally, discuss whether your different 'thoughts' leave any questions unanswered, and whether any of them will be helpful for people trying to make sense of their situation.

Source 1

Nothing occurs either in the earth, or in yourselves,
Without its being in a Book before We make it
happen.
That is something easy for Allah.
That is so that you will not be grieved
about the things that pass you by,
or exult about the things that come to you.

Surah 57:22

The Qur'an

Source 2

'Qadar (divine destiny) is one of the six articles of
faith for Muslims. It's the belief that Allah is the
creator, knower and controller of all things. Before
anything was created, Allah knew its destiny and
wrote it down. Nothing happens that isn't his
doing. This means that submitting to Allah's will
is really about accepting whatever happens to us,
good or bad, because we know it is the will of Allah.'

Activity 1

1 Each person should get a small piece of card or
strip of paper and write down one thing that could
cause suffering. It can be an everyday thing that
is pretty minor, or a bigger more serious thing. You
could use these examples to get you started, or
something from the posters you made at the start
of the section.

- It rains for a week; your house is flooded and
  you are left homeless.
- You fail one of your Unit Assessments for RMPS.
- You break your leg while skiing.
- Someone steals your new smart phone.
- You are diagnosed with a serious illness.
- A school bully has started picking on you.
- You are knocked down by a car.
- There is a bomb attack on your town which kills
  several people and leaves many injured.

Put the examples in a bag or box and then draw
them out, one at a time. As you draw out each
one, discuss: Does the belief in Qadar offer a full
explanation for the example you've been looking
at? Do you think the belief in Qadar leaves Muslims with any lingering questions about suffering
or about the nature of Allah? Might this belief affect how a Muslim feels about the choices people
make in life?

Write down any questions raised by your discussion on note cards (one per card) and share them.
Keep them handy for the next activity.

2 'Qadar means we just have to accept what
happens to us, good or bad.' Write a personal
response to this statement. Think about whether
it is easy to live like this. Are there advantages or
disadvantages to learning to just accept whatever
life throws at you? Share your responses with each
other.

3 Many Muslim thinkers and writers have written
about Qadar to try to help followers to understand
what it means. Spend some time online
looking at articles. See if they all offer the same

interpretation, and make a note of any important differences. Do any of them help to answer the questions you came up with? If you can, match any answers you find with the questions you wrote down on the note cards.

Source 3

Qadar is one explanation Muslims give for the existence of evil and suffering, and for some Muslims it's all they need. They would argue that it's wrong to ask 'Why?' when we see suffering because that is questioning Allah's will. For others, though, it's not quite so straightforward, and this is because of what Islam has to say about the nature of human beings and the universe.

The Pakistan earthquake of 2005 killed more than 75,000 people and injured more than 100,000

Source 4

Tom	So, absolutely everything that happens is a result of Allah's will?
Soraya	Yes, it has to be, or we would be denying the truth about Allah's nature.
Tom	I can see why people might want to say Allah is responsible for the nice stuff that happens to them, but you seem to be saying that he's responsible for all the horrible stuff too. If Allah is good, why would he want wars, disease, famines and floods? Isn't that a contradiction?
Soraya	Not if you see free will as part of divine destiny too. It's Allah's will that human beings have freedom to make decisions about how to act, otherwise we'd just be like robots. This means that we have the potential to cause a lot of good, but also a lot of suffering in the world. No one forces a person to be mean and nasty, or kind and caring.
Tom	OK, so Allah (who is good), created people with free will. Free will is a good thing, but it can be misused, and when it is, the result is often pain and suffering. That means human beings have to take some responsibility for suffering too.
Soraya	Yes. Allah knows every decision I'm ever going to make, and even whether I'll end up in Paradise or Hell, but I don't have that knowledge, so the choices I make are real and free, and that means I do have a say in my destiny. Yes, the future is already decided from Allah's point of view, but that's because he isn't stuck in time and space like we are.
Tom	But free will isn't enough to explain all the suffering in the world. What about natural disasters? Can they really be part of Allah's will too?

Activity 2

1 Use classroom and online resources to investigate some Islamic ideas about the *purpose* of suffering and evil. Arrange the information you find under headings like: punishment, testing, purifying, laws of nature. You can do this in groups or on your own, but either way make a careful note of your findings.

2 Using what you've found, either:

Continue the conversation between Tom and Soraya in the form of a script. You could then act it out for the rest of the class. Try to think about the questions Tom might have as well as the answers Soraya might offer.

OR

Produce an information leaflet with the title 'Suffering: a blessing in disguise'. It should be pitched at young Muslims, and should aim to give them some helpful answers to difficult questions raised by suffering and evil.

3 Discuss the importance of Allah's 'point of view' for Muslims who believe that people have real free will. Look back at Source 1. Does it support Soraya's view?

Source 5

Muslims believe that Allah created three kinds of being. Angels were created from pure light. The Qur'an also speaks about beings who are made of fire, and they are known to Muslims as 'jinn'. The most famous member of the jinn race is Iblis (sometimes called Satan). At first Iblis wanted to be with the angels and spent his time in worship and devotion to Allah. But when Allah formed human beings out of clay, everything changed.

Pilgrims throwing stones at pillars (representing the devil) in Mina, outside Mecca

Activity 3

1 Get a copy of the Qur'an (you can find translations online if you don't have a copy handy) and read Surah 15:26–40, Surah 7:10–26 and Surah 6:164–165. Look at the following statements and discuss whether you think they are true or false from a Muslim point of view. Try to explain your choice by referring to the passages you have read, and your previous work on Islam.

- Satan is real.
- People are really just clay.
- Satan should take some of the blame for suffering and evil.
- A good God couldn't have created Satan.
- Allah knew Iblis would rebel.
- Allah shouldn't have granted Iblis a reprieve.
- It would have been better if Allah hadn't given free will to human beings.

2 Find out how Iblis and other evil jinn are thought to try to lead Muslims astray. Then watch some video of Muslims 'stoning the devil' during the annual Hajj pilgrimage. What are Muslims showing as they take part in the ritual?

3 Most Muslims believe Satan is an actual being, but some prefer to think of him as a symbolic being. If Satan isn't real, how might the idea still be useful? What could Satan represent?

Activity 4

In groups, use a range of resources to research and create a presentation about the Islamic response to suffering. You should include:
- Muslim teachings about the importance of helping people who are suffering
- practical ways in which Muslims are working to help suffering people in the world today.

Activity 1

Take a quick class poll. How many people like the idea of being reincarnated after they die? How many don't? Share your reasons with each other.

Do you think you would get a different answer if you gave the same question to someone who lived in a slum where they had to scavenge for food every day, and where there was no clean water, or access to health care?

Source 1

'It still surprises me when my non-Hindu friends say they think reincarnation sounds like a brilliant idea. They clearly haven't understood what it really means. For one thing, it isn't "you" that gets reincarnated. It's the eternal atman (or soul), which is basically just catching a ride in your body during its short time on Earth. When your life is done, the atman leaves and catches a ride in a new body. "You" cease to exist. It's a bit like changing trains lots of times on an incredibly long and difficult journey. The cycle of birth, life, death and rebirth is called samsara, and for Hindus it's a horrible trap for the soul. Why a trap? Because while the soul is stuck in its many lives, it has to endure pain and suffering, every single time. Is it any wonder that the ultimate aim of Hinduism is to liberate the soul from samsara?'

Shiva Nataraja

Activity 2

1 In groups, get a large sheet of paper and on one side list some things that you think people get attached to in life. They can be material things, but also experiences and emotions. Compare your ideas and then circle any which you think will ultimately (in the end) lead to pain or suffering. Next to the ones you've circled, write a brief explanation for your decision. Are any of the things on your list left? Why did you decide not to circle them? Share your conclusions with another group.

Source 2

'The problem is that when a soul finds itself in a new body, it gets really attached to its life. There's just so much that appeals to our senses and our emotions that we want more and more and we cling on to it. We quickly forget that none of it lasts, and that it's really only the atman that matters. In the end our attachment to things can only lead to disappointment and pain. You'd think this undeniable truth would be obvious to people, but we all just carry on in a weird state of denial, and this keeps our souls stuck in samsara and makes it really hard to escape.'

2 Get a write-on copy of an image of the Hindu god Shiva Nataraja. There are a few things to notice:

- Around him is the circle of life.
- One hand says 'Stop!' (He's asking you to pay attention.)
- The other hand points to his raised foot, showing it is possible to escape from the cycle.
- Under the other foot he is crushing Apasmara, the demon of ignorance. He's saying that ignorance needs to be defeated if you want to escape the cycle.

Label your copy of the image to show what it is teaching. Look at Source 2 and discuss how ignorance can lead to suffering.

3 Spend some time researching the Hindu idea of ignorance (Avidya) and its connection to suffering. What kind of knowledge should Hindus be trying to get? Think about how you would explain your findings to a non-Hindu.

Source 3

It's obvious! We know that everything we do has consequences. Good actions have good consequences and bad actions have bad consequences, like doing well in a test because you bothered to revise, or getting punched on the nose because you started a fight. So, when people suffer it's because of their bad actions, and that's karma!

Amar

But isn't it also obvious that people don't always get what they deserve? I mean, we can all think of really good people who have incredibly tough lives, and rotten people who seem to sail through life with no problems at all. Life's just not fair, so how does karma explain that?

Kirsten

Source 4

The ability to make decisions for ourselves rather than just following our natural drive gives humans special status: we have free will, but with free will comes responsibility. You can't blame a tiger if it kills a deer, but if a man kills another out of greed, delusion or hatred it results in very serious karmic consequences. Then again, if a person selflessly helps others, superb karmic results will follow. We can lose our human status, Hindu sages warn. If we don't take advantage of our human birth but continue living like animals, we may return to an animal body in our next life.

Adapted from Linda Johnsen, *The Complete Idiot's Guide to Hinduism*

Activity 3

1 *'Life's just not fair!'* Do you agree with Kirsten (Source 3, page 119)? Think, pair and share your own views. You may want to think of some examples of ways in which karma *doesn't* seem to catch up with people. How would the Hindu sages mentioned in Source 4 argue that life *is* fair? What do you think the 'superb karmic results' could be? Write Amar's reply to Kirsten.

2 Dharma is the way a Hindu is meant to live; it's a bit like the prescription for generating positive karma.

   ■ Some dharma is shared by everyone.
   ■ Some depends on the group you were born into (Varnadharma).
   ■ Some depends on your stage in life (Ashramadharma).

   Split into five groups and research the dharma of one of the main groups in Hinduism. Prepare a short presentation for the class on the group you have researched.

3 Some groups seem to be destined to have a tougher life than others. Read Krishna's advice to Arjuna in the Bhagavad Gita 18:41–48. What would he say to someone who was struggling with their dharma?

4 *'If people are suffering, it's their own fault. Why should I get involved?'* How would a Hindu respond to this question? Spend some time in groups researching what Hinduism says about the right way to respond to the suffering of others. Present your findings to the rest of the class.

5 The samsara cycle: blessing or curse? Divide into two groups. One half of the class should suggest reasons why someone might say the samsara cycle is a good thing for Hindus, and the other side should suggest why Hindus might see it as a bad thing.

A Moksha Chitram board

Create

The board game Snakes and Ladders probably originated in India (its Indian name is Moksha Chitram) and it was designed to show how a soul can experience ups and downs on its journey through samsara.

In groups, create your own board game based on what you have learned about karma, dharma and samsara. It should be designed to teach young Hindus about the part they can play in their destiny. Is the luck of the dice the best way to determine progress through the game, or might there be a better way? You'll also need to ask: Will one board suit all Hindus, or is the game different for each varna? What shape should the board be: a square, a circle or even a spiral?

Source 5

'What's God got to do with suffering? Well, Hindus certainly think Brahman gets involved. There are loads of stories about Brahman taking on forms and coming to Earth to help out when people get into trouble, like when Krishna lifted up a hill on his pinkie to make a massive umbrella for his friends to shelter under during a storm. Hindus call the way God interacts with the world *lila*. It means "play", so you'd probably expect it to be a bit of harmless carrying on, but when the supreme reality plays, it can be catastrophic for the world. Sometimes those interactions result in what we think of as natural disasters: earthquakes, floods, tsunamis and the like.'

Activity 4

1 **Discuss:** Insurance companies refer to some of the bad things that happen to people as 'acts of God'. Are they saying God sometimes makes people suffer? If Brahman is everything, is 'the play of the gods' just another way of talking about 'the laws of physics'? Make a list of pros and cons of thinking about Brahman in this way.

2 Atheists sometimes argue that the terrible suffering we see in nature means a good God can't exist. Do you think Hindus can offer a helpful response to this view?

3 Some Hindu thinkers believe it's wrong to bring God into an explanation for why people suffer. Some prefer to talk about 'collective karma'. Do you think it's right to say people can collectively generate negative consequences for the world? How might systems and structures in modern society add to human suffering? Does this mean it's right to say life is not fair after all?

How does Buddhism explain the existence of suffering?

Source 1

A story

Once upon a time there was a handsome prince. His parents, the king and queen, loved him very much, and they couldn't bear the thought of him seeing anything upsetting or unpleasant. So, they decided to keep him safely in the palace, well away from anything that could spoil his perfect life. The queen used make-up to disguise her wrinkles as she got older, and the king ordered the gardener to dig up flowers and replace them with new ones before they started to droop. Although the prince had a brilliant life, he couldn't help wondering about what it was like for people who lived outside the palace, so one day he sneaked outside without telling his parents. As he walked through the village he saw four things that would completely change his life: an elderly man was shuffling along, bent over with age; another man sat outside his house moaning in pain because of a nasty disease; a group of people were crying over the body of a loved one who had died. Then he saw a holy man, who had devoted his life to trying to make sense of it all, and he knew he was going to spend the rest of his life doing the same. The prince's name was Siddartha Gautama, but he would become known as the Buddha.

Activity 1

1   Divide the story of The Four Sights into key scenes and then split into groups to each produce one panel for a frieze or a big cartoon strip retelling it. (There are different versions of the story, so check a few out for more ideas.) Assemble the frieze or cartoon strip and display it.

2   Discuss what happened to Gautama when he left the palace, and what he learned from the experience. What had he discovered about the kinds of things that cause suffering? Who is affected by suffering?

3   Gautama knew he could never go back to his comfortable life. Should he have tried to return to the palace? Would it have been better if he had never left in the first place?

4   Find out what Gautama did after leaving the palace. How did he go about trying to make sense of what he had seen? You might want to add to your frieze or cartoon strip.

Prince Siddartha Gautama and the four sights

Source 2

'I find it most helpful to think of the Buddha like a doctor. After he realised that something was terribly wrong with the world, he spent many years trying to reach a diagnosis. His observation of his own life and the lives of those around him showed that suffering is an undeniable fact of life, and that it comes to each and every one of us. It's the "sickness" we all share. So, he set out to identify its cause in order to try to come up with a cure.'

Source 3

Sure, suffering includes the big stuff like illness, death and disaster, but Buddha came to understand that it's much, much more. Suffering includes anything about life that leaves us anxious, disappointed or dissatisfied. It's that sense we all get that our happiness is temporary, and that in the end nothing lasts. The word that Buddhists use for this general 'unsatisfactoriness', as well as the obvious stuff, is dukkha.

Activity 2

1. Discuss: Is Buddhism right? Is suffering a fact of life for everyone?
2. Do you think it's right to include the everyday things that cause us disappointment in life in a description of suffering?

   Think about these examples:
   - Your boy/girl friend forgets to phone you.
   - You drop your new smartphone and scratch the cover.
   - You find a hole in the elbow of your favourite jumper.
   - You stub your toe on the leg of a table.
   - Your numbers don't come up in the lottery ... again.
   - You are made to eat Brussels sprouts (even though they make you feel sick).

   In one minute, list as many things as you can think of that *don't* ultimately (in the end) lead to disappointment.

3. Find out about the three different kinds of dukkha in Buddhism, and make a note of your findings (you'll need them to help you make a diagnosis

later). Discuss what Buddhists might say about the list you made for Task 2.

4. *'Buddhism has a very negative view of life.'* From what you've looked at so far, do you think this is true?

Source 4

Kate So suffering is just an inevitable part of existing?

Annie Yep; it's something we just can't escape.

Kate Not much hope for a cure then?

Annie Not at all! Buddha went on to see if he could figure out what the underlying cause was, and whether he could do anything about it.

Kate What did he discover?

Annie That suffering is really all in the mind. It's our ignorance, anger and attachment to impermanent things that leads to dukkha.

Kate Which means the cure would have to be in the mind too; I'm guessing getting a better understanding, remaining calm and trying not to get attached to things.

Annie Exactly, but the cure involves the body too. You see, what's going on in our minds usually ends up affecting our behaviour, so the prescription includes right action as well as right attitudes.

Kate That's all very well, but how *do* we know what the right actions and attitudes are?

Annie Buddha told us that too, and he summarised it in what's become known as 'The Noble Eightfold Path'.

The Buddhist wheel of life

Activity 3

1. In groups or pairs, divide a large paper circle into eight equal sections (like a cake sliced into eight pieces). Research what's involved in the Noble Eightfold Path and write a summary of each step in the slices.

2. Find a copy of the story of Kisa Gotami and read it together. In groups discuss: Which of the three kinds of dukkha was Kisa Gotami suffering from? What was Buddha's 'prescription'? Which of the steps of the Noble Eightfold Path do you think would be particularly helpful for Kisa Gotami?

3. Look back at the examples of suffering and evil you collected at the start of this section. How many of them would be eliminated if everyone managed to follow Buddha's prescription? Does what you've looked at so far leave any aspects of suffering unexplained?

4. Finally, look back at your answer to Task 4 in Activity 2. Has your view changed? Try to explain your answer.

Members of the Chinese Buddhist Tzu Chi Foundation distributing relief aid in Marikina, after typhoons in the Philippines, 2009

Source 5

'As a Buddhist, I believe the natural law of cause and effect is enough to explain everything that happens in the world. We see cause and effect all the time in nature, for example when the Earth's tectonic plates shift, causing earthquakes and tsunamis. Our attitudes, words and actions have effects too, but while we have to accept that we have no control over the forces of nature, we can control how we behave, and this means that we need to take responsibility for the results. The word Buddhists use for human attitudes, words and actions, as well as their effects, is kamma. All our actions have an effect, but not all effects are due to our actions.'

Activity 4

1. Buddhists don't believe in God, and they don't think God is necessary to help explain suffering and evil. From Source 5, can you explain why this is?

2. If following the Noble Eightfold Path can't prevent suffering in things like natural disasters, might it help people to cope when they do happen? Suggest five ways in which a Buddhist's response to suffering might have positive kammic results, and five ways in which it might lead to negative kammic results.

3. From what you've learned so far, where do you think a Buddhist would put the X on the freedom scale you used in Chapter 36? Could a Buddhist increase their amount of free will by following Buddha's prescription?

4. 'Rebirth' is an important idea in Buddhism. Use class and online resources to produce a Q&A sheet which gives answers to the following questions (you can include others if you want to). Your sheet should be aimed at someone who doesn't know anything about Buddhism.

   - What do Buddhists mean by 'rebirth'?
   - What is the relationship between kamma and rebirth?
   - What is the relationship between rebirth and suffering?
   - Is there any hope of escaping the cycle of rebirth?

5. Finally, have a go at doing the last task in the Christianity section (see Chapter 37, headed **Create**), but this time from a Buddhist point of view.

Source 1

'When people do science they systematically study the natural, material world. It stands to reason that they will be able to offer some insight into why there is suffering. A cancer researcher will explain how normal cells begin to grow in an uncontrolled way; a volcanologist will describe the sequence of events leading up to a volcanic eruption. It's all just cause and effect. But if you ask them to explain what God has to do with it, or if there is a greater purpose or meaning behind suffering, they'll most likely say, "You'd better ask someone else. We don't do the why questions".'

Source 2

The total amount of suffering per year in the natural world is beyond all decent contemplation. During the minute that it takes me to compose this sentence, thousands of animals are being eaten alive, many others are running for their lives, whimpering with fear, others are slowly being devoured from within by rasping parasites, thousands of all kinds are dying of starvation, thirst, and disease. It must be so. If there ever is a time of plenty, this very fact will automatically lead to an increase in the population until the natural state of starvation and misery is restored. In a universe of electrons and selfish genes, blind physical forces and genetic replication, some people are going to get hurt, other people are going to get lucky, and you won't find any rhyme or reason in it, nor any justice. The universe that we observe has precisely the properties we should expect if there is, at bottom, no design, no purpose, no evil, no good, nothing but pitiless indifference.

Professor Richard Dawkins, *River out of Eden*

Activity 2

1 List some more 'how' questions science has answered in relation to suffering and evil. Try to give examples of things in nature *and* in human nature that science has explained (you can include discoveries in things like psychology and neuroscience).

2 What does Source 1 mean by 'why' questions? Why might science be unable to help with these kinds of questions? If science can't answer them, should we bother asking them?

3 Richard Dawkins is a materialist. This means he believes that the material world of stuff is all there is. Do you agree that the nature of stuff is enough to explain evil and suffering? Would a materialist consider asking someone else to answer the 'why' questions?

4 Do you think religious people could agree with any of Sources 1 and 2? What bits would they disagree with? Does it depend on their religion?

5 Is it possible that the universe we observe is one which has the properties we should expect if it *was* designed for a purpose by a good God? Write a letter to Professor Dawkins from the point of view of someone who thinks it is.

6 Do you think there could be free will in the kind of universe Dawkins describes?

Source 3

I am very comfortable with the idea that we can override biology with free will. Indeed, I encourage people all the time to do it. Much of the message of my first book, *The Selfish Gene*, was that we must understand what it means to be … programmed by genes, so that we are better equipped to escape, so that we are better equipped to use our big brains, use our conscious intelligence, to depart from the dictates of the selfish genes and to build for ourselves a new kind of life which as far as I am concerned the more un-Darwinian it is the better, because the Darwinian world in which our ancestors were selected is a very unpleasant world. Nature really is red in tooth and claw. And when we sit down together to argue out and discuss and decide upon how we want to run our societies, I think we should hold up Darwinism as an awful warning for how we should not organise our societies.

Professor Richard Dawkins, www.pbs.org/faithandreason/transcript/dawk-body.html

Professor Richard Dawkins

Activity 3

1   Try to explain in your own words why Dawkins believes we do have free will.

2   In Source 2 Dawkins says he doesn't believe there is good or evil *behind* the universe. What do you think he means? Do you think he believes there is good and evil *in* the universe?

3   Find out a bit more about how a Darwinian world works by looking at Chapter 23 in 'The origins of life' section of this book.

4   If Dawkins is right, do you think there's hope for a world with less suffering in it?

5   Some scientists disagree with Richard Dawkins; they think free will is impossible because everything that happens is determined. You've looked at this already, so see how much of the argument you can remember without looking back. Give yourself one minute to write down the main points individually, then share your answers before checking to see how much you got right.

6   Spend some time researching the views of Susan Blackmore. She's a psychologist who believes that free will is a total illusion. Create a poster or presentation to show her main ideas.

Source 4

'Religious people will argue that suffering is God's way of testing or punishing people. They might say it's part of his good plan, or that humans cause suffering because they have inherited the "disease" of sin from Adam and Eve. As a humanist, none of this makes sense to me, because I don't think it's reasonable to believe in God. When it comes to the problem of evil and suffering, I believe we're on our own. God doesn't explain it, and he isn't going to fix it either. So, instead of trying to make sense of a non-existent God, we should turn our attention to human beings and ask what part we can play in addressing the very real problem of evil and suffering.'

www.humanism.org.uk
www.richarddawkins.net
www.atheistcampaign.org

Source 5

Some Humanist beliefs:

- Human beings are part of nature.
- Human beings can use reason and make rational decisions.
- Human beings can think about the consequences of their actions.
- Human beings can use their imagination to understand how others feel.
- Human beings should respect the rights and freedoms of others.
- Human beings have the capacity for both good and evil.
- Human beings have free will (with limits).
- Most human beings do good; only a few do really evil things.
- Human beings are the world's only hope.

Based on an article from www.humanism.org.uk

Activity 3

1 Humanists tend to accept the findings of science, so they would agree that some suffering is just down to the laws of physics, but Humanism is also concerned with questions about how people can live moral lives. Using the information in Sources 4 and 5, list some ways in which human beings could be seen as a) the cause of and b) the solution to suffering.

2 Take each of the points in Source 5 and discuss whether religious people would agree with them.

3 'Instead of calling people evil, we should try to understand why people do evil things.' Are Humanists right? Try to explain why you agree or disagree with the statement. If human beings are 'part of nature' do you think we could one day get a complete explanation for why people cause pain and suffering?

Religious and non-religious views: is there common ground?

Source 6

Karen Armstrong is an ex-nun and theologian. She thought she was done with religion, but her studies led her to realise that, while religions seem to cause a lot of pain in the world, they also offer a solution, and it's a solution that many non-religious people believe in too.

In 2008 she won the prestigious TED Prize for a talk which challenged people to 'activate the golden rule' in the world. Since then, the Charter for Compassion has become a global movement.

Activity 4

1 Spend some time exploring the Charter online (you can find her talk at **www.TED.com**). Discuss whether it has anything to offer in a world full of suffering and evil. How much of the Charter could be adopted by both religious *and* non-religious people? Are there any drawbacks to trying to live in the way that the Charter describes?

2 Gather some stories from within (and beyond) your class, of ways in which people have shown or been shown compassion. Share them with each other and display them for others to read.

3 Finally, discuss how your work on this section has affected your own thinking about the problem of suffering and evil, whether it can be explained, and whether there is anything we humans should be doing about it.

This section has given you the opportunity to explore a range of views on the question, 'If God is good, why do people suffer?'

If you're doing the N5 exam, you'll be asked to show that you understand ideas about **God's nature**, and **free will and responsibility** as well as religious or non-religious views about these ideas.

You will also be expected to show that you can write about the strengths and weaknesses of the different views, and their impact on people's lives today.

Unlike a lot of assessments, the exam won't ask for specific viewpoints, so you will need to decide how to apply what you've learned.

Now try using what you've done in this section to answer the following exam-style questions.

Exam-style questions

1 Explain what a religious person might mean by 'suffering'. **(4 KU)**

2 Explain how suffering and evil could challenge a person's belief about God. **(6 KU)**

3 *'It's important for me to have an explanation for the bad stuff that happens to people.'* **Jane**

   Give **two** reasons why Jane might say this. **(4 KU)**

4 Choose a religious viewpoint you have studied. Explain what it says about the nature of God. **(5 KU)**

5 Explain how belief in a good God could affect a person in their daily life. **(4 SKILLS)**

6 *'God can't be good. Suffering proves it!'* Do you agree? Give reasons for your answer. **(8 SKILLS)**

7 Choose a non-religious view you have studied. Explain what it says about the causes of suffering. **(6 KU)**

8 (a) Explain what someone might mean by 'free will'. **(6 KU)**

   (b) *'Free will gives a complete explanation for suffering.'* Would religious people agree? Give reasons for your answer. **(8 SKILLS)**

9 Explain some possible consequences of believing that people do **not** have free will. **(4 SKILLS)**

10 Compare two religious viewpoints on the reason for suffering. **(8 SKILLS)**

11 *'When it comes to understanding the reasons for suffering, religious and non-religious people have nothing in common.'* Is this true? Give reasons for your answer. **(8 SKILLS)**